The Elements of Spreadsheet Style

Also by John M. Nevison

The Little Book of Basic Style: How to Write a Program You Can Use
Executive Computing: How to Get It Done on Your Own
Executive Computing: How to Get It Done with Spreadsheets and Graphs

The Elements of Spreadsheet Style

John M. Nevison

A Brady Book
Published by Prentice Hall Press
New York, New York 10023

A Brady Book
Published by Prentice Hall Press
A Division of Simon & Schuster, Inc.
Gulf + Western Building
One Gulf + Western Plaza
New York, New York 10023

PRENTICE HALL PRESS is a trademark of Simon & Schuster, Inc.

Manufactured in the United States of America

1 2 3 4 5 6 7 8 9 10

Library of Congress Cataloging-in-Publication Data

Nevison, John M.
　The elements of spreadsheet style.

　"A Brady Book."
　Bibliography: p.
　Includes index.
　1. Electronic spreadsheets. 2. Business—
Data processing. I. Title.
HF5548.2.N416　1987　　　　005.3　　　　87-6922
ISBN 0-13-080565-3

To Susannah, Laura, and Nancy

C O N T E N T S

P R E F A C E

Writing a good spreadsheet requires the kind of careful thought you would devote to writing a good letter. Editing either document demands further patient attention. The purpose of this small book is to help you write and edit a spreadsheet. William Strunk once wrote a book on how to write clear English. E. B. White added a section on style and republished the book as *The Elements of Style*. The present book takes its title and inspiration from their book. The rules are short, the discussion is limited, and the examples are simple in the hope that the ideas will be easy to read and reread.

THE NEED FOR RULES OF STYLE

The need for rules of style extends beyond the technology. A word processor cannot make a good writer, nor can a spreadsheet program make a sound analyst. There is no technological fix for sloppy thought or poor expression. You need to know that writing a good spreadsheet is hard work; that this work can be rewarding and fulfilling, and that the rules of style in this book can help you to do this work well.

These twenty-two rules are not intended to set brittle standards of performance; they are intended to encourage you, the spreadsheet author, to think seriously about the purpose of your work. All spreadsheets must first be correct. If they are to maintain this correctness over time, they must be clear. If they are to maintain this correctness when they are modified by others, they must be clear and well structured.

If these rules help you form the habits of careful spreadsheet construction, of reflection and revision, of precision and focus, they will dramatically enhance your professional productivity.

The examples that accompany the rules show weak and strong versions of the ideas in practice. The terms *weak* and *strong* were chosen to indicate that these are merely examples on a continuum: other examples might be worse than the weak or better than the strong. As you work on your spreadsheets, you very well may improve on the examples provided here.

NOVICE READER, EXPERIENCED READER

If you are new to spreadsheets, before you use this book you must learn your particular tool, be it 1-2-3 ™, Excel™, or another of the many spreadsheets available today. You must know how to build and copy formulas, how to move areas about on the spreadsheet, whether your program has a graphics ability, and, if it does, how it works. You may find parts of this book helpful without knowing your tool, but you will want to read the rules again after you have mastered your own particular spreadsheet program. In short, you should know something about your paints and brushes before you begin to explore the problems of composing a picture.

As a novice spreadsheet user, *please follow the rule before you break it.* After you use an apparently inconvenient rule on a few spreadsheets, you may find it has become an absolute necessity. You may also find that because you do not have to unlearn a lot of bad habits your work may quickly achieve a higher standard than that of your more experienced colleagues.

If you are an experienced user of spreadsheets you may have difficulty with some of the rules in this book. However, if you strongly disagree with a rule, it should be for the same reason that the rule was advanced: because there is a better way to build a clear, correct spreadsheet. Few, if any, experienced readers will agree with all of the rules, but every experienced reader will find at least one new rule that will improve his or her spreadsheets. That one rule will repay the cost of the book and the effort of reading it.

As all readers become experienced they should heed the other, unwritten rule: *When you have a good reason, break the rule.* Rules should encourage thoughtful activity, not pigheaded subservience.

PARTICULAR SPREADSHEET PROGRAMS

The spreadsheets in this book are intended to be *generic,* and they will run as shown on almost all spreadsheet programs. Some of the spreadsheets that appear here were first written in VisiCalc™, many have been written in 1-2-3™, and all were written in Jazz™. Every spreadsheet feature that appears here is available in 1-2-3™ and Excel™. The features that support graphing, macros, and databases will vary from one spreadsheet to the next. You may overcome this variation by applying the idea behind a rule to your own particular examples. The formulas in this book have all been presented in 1-2-3™ format—for example, @SUM instead of SUM—to make them familiar to the broadest possible audience.

NURSERY RHYMES

The nursery rhymes in the book are intended to relieve the somewhat sober nature of the subject. Rhymes that are puzzles introduce some of the chapters. Rhymes about historical personages appear in the text and have dates that loosely correspond to the person about whom the rhyme was written. For example, in the spreadsheet Sixpence, the King is Henry VIII, the Queen is Catherine of Aragon, the maid is Anne Boleyn (who eventually had her head, not just her nose, snapped off), and the blackbird is Cardinal Wolsey; the date is 1536, an arbitrary year during the reign of Henry VIII. Mary, Queen of Scots, figures in several rhymes, and so does Queen Elizabeth I. Other English royalty can be guessed by the dates. For those who like historical puzzles, Humpty Dumpty's spreadsheet contains the only actual historical date in the book. The date on the spreadsheets ascribed to Mother Goose herself (she has no known tie to an historical personage) is 1386, the year when Chaucer is believed to have begun his *Canterbury Tales*.

ACKNOWLEDGEMENTS

The ideas that began the journey toward this book arose in discussions with John Kenower, Tim Stein, and Julie Bingham. These ideas were given their first field tests in courses at CIGNA Corporation and at the Boston Edison Company. Students contributed ideas in other classes taught at Arco, CBS, Chesebrough-Pond's, Coca-Cola, GTE, Gillette, General Electric, Lotus, Mellon Bank, and Westinghouse. The manuscript profited from the careful reading of Jim Chelini, Joe Gwinn, Bill Schillhammer, Steve Shapse, and Tim Stein. Michael Vitale of the Harvard Business School and Ted Standish of the Gillette Company had kind words when they were needed most. Michael O'Brien of Brady gave the manuscript the critical reading it needed (and a new Rule 12). Milissa Koloski and Terry Anderson, also of Brady, remained patient and good-humored in the face of several delays. My two daughters, Laura and Susannah, made the work more fun by crawling into my lap and providing needed interruptions. My final and largest debt of gratitude is to my wife, Nancy Ross McJennett, who protected my working time so well that I was embarrassed to have no real excuse for procrastination. The mistakes that remain are unavoidably the responsibility of the author.

John M. Nevison
Concord, MA
June 1987

1

INTRODUCTION: FORM FOLLOWS FUNCTION

Every lady in this land
Has twenty nails, upon each hand
Five, and twenty on hands and feet:
All this is true, without deceit.

A spreadsheet should be of good character. It should be straightforward to build, easy to read, simple to use, receptive to change, and, above all, free of error.

The first step towards achieving this goal is to construct a spreadsheet that has an *appropriate form*. This form is the cornerstone of correctness. When each function is carried out in an appropriate location, its activity can be verified by eye and reviewed by a thoughtful reader. The appropriate form also denies errors a place to hide. When something is out of place, it looks out of place.

Because the appropriate form focuses your attention on the proper detail at the proper place, it is easy to remember and you do not get lost. A user engaged in the small changes of normal use knows where to alter an initial "what if" assumption, where to slip in a new calculation, and where to modify a printed report.

When a spreadsheet must undergo a major overhaul to meet a new need, the appropriate form will suggest where you can make the additions and deletions.

Finally, the appropriate form not only reveals the completed thought, it supports and guides the unfolding thought. A completed spreadsheet often can be reused as a template for subsequent work. Such a template saves a significant amount of start-up time on a new project, ensures that you will not forget an important section of the spreadsheet, and provides a guiding framework for thinking about the problem under examination.

A SONG OF SIXPENCE

To understand what this appropriate form might look like in practice, consider the spreadsheet model below.

	Income	Rent	Tax	Poor tax	Real inc.
King	90000	15000	20700	180	54120
Queen	75000	12000	17250	180	45570
Maid	12000	1000	2760	180	8060
Blackbird	3000	200	690	180	1930
Totals	180000	28200	41400	720	109680

While it is small, it raises several questions. Who wrote it? What is its name? When was it written? What is its purpose? Why is it so hard to read? Is it complete? Is it accurate?

Now take a look at a second version of the same model.

Twopence   10 December 1536   King Henry

To show how income is distributed in the kingdom.

KINGDOM INCOME DISTRIBUTION 1537

Person	Income	Rent	Tax	Poor tax	Real inc.
King	90,000	15,000	20,700	180	54,120
Queen	75,000	12,000	17,250	180	45,570
Maid	12,000	1,000	2,760	180	8,060
Blackbird	3,000	200	690	180	1,930
Totals	180,000	28,200	41,400	720	109,680

Twopence is a clear improvement. You know its name, when it was created, and by whom. You have been thrust into a nursery rhyme kingdom. You know the model's purpose: to show how income is distributed in the kingdom. The results have been laid out in an easy-to-read fashion. You have some idea how this model might be used.

Yet this apparently complete version is not complete. Twopence is hiding information. While you expect a spreadsheet to work with formulas you can't see (for example, the totals row or the real income column), you do not want formulas to contain hidden numbers. Hidden numbers are buried threats. Unknown to the viewer and hard to find for the user, these concealed figures can sabotage the best-intentioned effort. In the case of Twopence the hidden number is the tax rate that is buried in the formulas in the tax column. You are being denied access to important information about this model. The third version reveals this small, but highly significant, detail.

Threepence   10 December 1536   King Henry

To show how income is distributed in the kingdom.

Assumptions: 23% Tax rate
                                         180 Poor tax
Model:
KINGDOM INCOME DISTRIBUTION 1537

Person	Income	Rent	Tax	Poor tax	Real inc.
King	90,000	15,000	20,700	180	54,120
Queen	75,000	12,000	17,250	180	45,570
Maid	12,000	1,000	2,760	180	8,060
Blackbird	3,000	200	690	180	1,930
Totals	180,000	28,200	41,400	720	109,680

Threepence tells you that the tax rate is 23 percent. Now what you see is what you get. All of the information on which the model depends is visible.

Notice that the poor tax appears as an assumption too. While it was visible before, it was repeated four times. Now, by appearing as an assumption and having the four occurrences in the model all tied to the assumption, the poor tax may be changed by changing only one number instead of four.

You can also change the tax rate for the whole model by changing one number, the 23 percent at the top of the model. In addition to making the information accessible, the visible assumptions allow you to *modify* the program without digging into the formulas.

For many purposes Threepence may be satisfactory. But if King Henry knows he will be off on a quest and wants to leave things in a fashion that will be easy for Queen Jane to handle, he might rearrange the model for another person to use.

Fourpence   10 December 1536   King Henry

To show how income is distributed in the kingdom.

Initial Data:

23%	Tax rate	
180	Poor tax	

Income	Person	Rent	Dwelling
90000	King	15000	Counting house
75000	Queen	12000	Parlor
12000	Maid	1000	Garden house
3000	Blackbird	200	Garden

Model:

KINGDOM INCOME DISTRIBUTION 1537

Person	Income	Rent	Tax	Poor tax	Real inc.
King	90,000	15,000	20,700	180	54,120
Queen	75,000	12,000	17,250	180	45,570
Maid	12,000	1,000	2,760	180	8,060
Blackbird	3,000	200	690	180	1,930
Totals	180,000	28,200	41,400	720	109,680

Fourpence extracts all the raw numbers from the model, collects them, and labels them in the initial data area near the top of the spreadsheet. Fourpence then changes all the numbers in the model area to formulas. For example, the King's 90,000 income down in the model is no longer a number; it is a one-term formula that refers to the raw value up in the initial data. All the apparent numbers in the model are formulas that refer to the raw values in the initial data or formulas that construct other values, such as the tax, from these numbers. Fourpence separates all the raw data from the formulas.

Having this separation allows a split in how the model is handled. The original author, the King, can work anywhere in the spreadsheet. But when he is finished, he can lock up the formulas in the model itself. The second user of the model, the Queen, never has to touch a formula. She may exercise the model by simply changing figures in the initial data. Providing an area for the initial data allows the raw data to be not only visible, but fully labeled. In this case, you find out that the parlor rents for $12,000, and you can infer that the Queen is there (eating bread and honey).

The King wants to prepare some clear, concise reports: one for the Queen on the spending of the royal funds and one for the Maid on the distribution of the royal burden. He extends his model to include these two reports.

Fivepence   10 December 1536   King Henry

To show how income is distributed in the kingdom.

Contents:

Initial data and beginning assumptions

23% Tax rate
180 Poor tax
1537 Year of report

Income	Person	Rent	Dwelling
90000	King	15000	Counting house
75000	Queen	12000	Parlor
12000	Maid	1000	Garden house
3000	Blackbird	200	Garden

Income distribution model

KINGDOM INCOME DISTRIBUTION   1537

Person	Income	Rent	Tax	Poor tax	Real inc.
King	90,000	15,000	20,700	180	54,120
Queen	75,000	12,000	17,250	180	45,570
Maid	12,000	1,000	2,760	180	8,060
Blackbird	3,000	200	690	180	1,930
Totals	180,000	28,200	41,400	720	109,680

Report on kingdom's spending for the year   1537

28,200	Funds for the maintainance of the buildings and grounds.
41,400	Funds for the defense of the kingdom
720	Funds for the poor
70,320	Total spent

Distribution of royal burden   1537

Person	Burden $	Burden as percentage of income %
King	35,880	40
Queen	29,430	39
Maid	3,940	33
Blackbird	1,070	36
	70,320	39

Now that the model has grown beyond what can be seen on one screen, the King has added a table of contents. The contents gives the reader a quick idea of the full extent of the model. The King also has added two new regions to the spreadsheet. Each region is intended to be a report that can be printed out independently of the rest of the model. By giving each report its own area, the King has made it easier for either report to be modified.

Because he wanted the year to appear in both reports as well as in his original model, he has added the year of the report to the initial data.

Looking at Fivepence you might wonder whether the whole effort has been overdone. Clearly, this model is more work than the already satisfactory Threepence. Is Fivepence worth the trouble? To answer this question, consider for a moment how it might be used.

Late in 1537 the King was away on a quest, and he wrote home to his Queen suggesting that they increase the tax rate to whatever was necessary to cover an anticipated 50,000 dollar expense in the defense of the Kingdom. The rye crop had been good, so the Queen knew everyone would receive an increase in their income. The Queen wanted to increase the poor tax, if she could do it without increasing the overall royal burden on the population.

The Queen called up Fivepence and:

1. Entered the new incomes: $100,000 for the king, $88,000 for the Queen, $15,000 for the Maid, and $4,500 for the Blackbird.
2. Held rents the same.
3. Increased the tax rate until the total tax exceeded $50,000.
4. Increased the poor tax until the overall burden equalled the previous year's burden.

When she was finished, she retitled the model Sixpence.

Sixpence   15 November 1537   Queen Jane

To show how income is distributed in the kingdom.

Contents:

INTRO	Introduction: Title, description, contents.
INITIAL	Initial data and beginning assumptions.
MODEL	Income distribution model.
REPORT1	Report on kingdom's spending for the year.
REPORT2	Distribution of royal burden.

Initial data and beginning assumptions

25%	Tax rate
471	Poor tax
1538	Year of report

Income	Person	Rent	Dwelling
100000	King	15000	Counting house
88000	Queen	12000	Parlor
15000	Maid	1000	Garden house
4500	Blackbird	200	Garden

Income distribution model

KINGDOM INCOME DISTRIBUTION 1538

Person	Income	Rent	Tax	Poor tax	Real inc.
King	100,000	15,000	25,000	471	59,529
Queen	88,000	12,000	22,000	471	53,529
Maid	15,000	1,000	3,750	471	9,779
Blackbird	4,500	200	1,125	471	2,704
Totals	207,500	28,200	51,875	1,884	125,541

Report on kingdom's spending for the year 1538

28,200	Funds for the maintenance of the buildings and grounds.
51,875	Funds for the defense of the kingdom
1,884	Funds for the poor
81,959	Total spent

Distribution of royal burden 1538

Person	Burden $	Burden as percentage of income %
King	40,471	40
Queen	34,471	39
Maid	5,221	35
Blackbird	1,796	40
	81,959	39

Because the structure of Fivepence made it convenient for a second person to use, the model was successfully integrated into the regular work habits of the administration. If the King set out to build a model to help rule the kingdom, he achieved his goal. The Queen could carry on in the King's absence.

What is the moral of these six versions? *Form follows function.* What form is appropriate depends on what function the spreadsheet is intended to fulfill. This does not mean all forms are adequate to some purpose. Onepence and Twopence are clearly unsatisfactory. Threepence, Fourpence, and Fivepence, however, each satisfy a different purpose. If you wish to have a personal model you can quickly build and change, then Threepence is fine. If you are going to let another person use your model, Fourpence is a sound approach. If you find that your model is composed of several parts, Fivepence is appropriate. Sixpence is evidence that Fivepence works.

To understand in more detail how spreadsheets should be fashioned you need to know the rules for the basic form and the rules for extensions to the basic form. With these rules you can fashion forms appropriate to your functions. The next three chapters will present twenty-two rules to get you started.

2

THE BASIC FORM

The basic form divides into three fundamental parts: the Introduction, where you tell the reader what is about to appear; the Initial Data Area, where you present the raw material of the model; and the Model Area, where the spreadsheet performs its work in an informative and attractive manner. Sometimes a spreadsheet may abbreviate one part, but every spreadsheet should have at least a line devoted to each of these three basic pieces.

INTRODUCTION

1. Make a formal introduction.

The top of the model introduces the reader to the model. Here the reader must get his bearings, and here the work of the spreadsheet is fit into larger contexts. The top ties the model to the outside world. Several devices each play introductory roles:

- the title line telegraphs critical information,
- the description declares the purpose,
- the directions say how to use the model,
- the references offer collateral information, and
- the table of contents maps the spreadsheet's organization.

By the time the reader leaves the introduction he should have a good idea of how the model fits into the activities of the real world and where to go in the model to explore the details.

2. Title to tell.

The first thing the reader encounters is the title of the model. Make it tell. It should be short, apt, and memorable. In conjunction with the first few lines of the introduction, the title should allow the reader to decide whether to quit or to continue. All of the remaining reading will be colored by the title's first impression. Make sure it is the right impression.

Weak	Strong		
Sim3x5	Pies	4 March 1620	S. Simon
Tuff13.6	Tuffet	15 May 1560	M. Muffet
Lost	Sheep	22 June 1563	B. Peep

The title line telegraphs critical information. A strong title line contains at least the name of the model, the date it was completed, and the person who wrote it. Plain names are more informative than abbreviations. Nouns or verbs tell more than adjectives.

Choosing the right name for your model is especially important when your model will immediately become the property of several people or must fit into an existing scheme of documents. Others can immediately identify how your contribution fits into the group effort if the name follows local convention. Suppose your model is the third one supporting a proposal to Acorn Corporation. One strong title might be:

Acorn Proposal #33 Model #3

But if it must fit in eight characters, it requires some abbreviation. Here is what one abbreviation might look like:

Weak	Strong
ACP33M03	ACP33M03 24 May 1488 T. Tucker
	Acorn Corporation Proposal 33, Model 3

Terse titles that follow an established abbreviation standard need a decoded explanation in the spreadsheet itself. The strong example shows how a two-line title can meet a terse naming standard and yet remain comprehensible to a busy reader. Naming conventions also need the support of:

- a list of the current conventions posted on the wall near every computer that will use these names,
- a regular, attentive review and update procedure, and
- a manager (called a librarian) to oversee the function.

There is no magic in having only one or two lines for the title. When the critical information grows to several lines to meet work demands, the title line can become a title area. The title area should be so familiar that it can be read like a title line. The title, line or area, should telegraph critical information.

Strong

NURSERY KINGDOM   CONFIDENTIAL INFORMATION

Name:	Silver Bells
Date:	12 August 1560
Author:	M. Contrary
Dept:	Garden
Division:	Outdoor
Date last modified:	23 Sept 1561
Last modified by:	M. Contrary

Several critical pieces of information appear in Silver Bells. The formal heading identifies the owner of the information and notifies the reader that this information is confidential. Not only do you have the name, date, and author, you know the department name, the division name, and the name of the corporation. On

August 12, 1560, Mary Contrary completed the spreadsheet Silver Bells while she was in the Garden Department of the Outdoor Division of the Nursery Kingdom.

A modification is also mentioned here. You know that Mary Contrary revised the model on September 23, 1561. Another style of doing the revision history could allow for the insertion of further updates.

Strong

NURSERY KINGDOM   CONFIDENTIAL INFORMATION

Name:	Silver Bells
Date:	12 August 1560
Author:	M. Contrary
Dept:	Garden
Division:	Outdoor

Date modified	Who modified and what
4 Nov 1561	M. Contrary added a row for pretty maids
23 Sept 1561	M. Contrary added a column for cockle shells

This modification format allows the reader to read the history of changes to the original spreadsheet. You can see that Mary most recently added a row for pretty maids and before that a column of cockle shells. If the spreadsheet starts to misbehave when you use it, you have some strong hints where to begin looking for recently introduced errors. When the modification history grows unwieldy, you should write a new version of the spreadsheet and revise the entire introduction.

3. Declare the model's purpose.

The model's purpose should be immediately available to the reader. He or she needs to know that his or her purposes and the spreadsheet's are similar. After becoming aware of what the model intends to achieve, the reader needs to have some idea how the model will achieve it. This does not require a lengthy description, just a clear one. The model's intentions should be honorable and clearly stated.

Weak	Strong
Set of accounts on the King's travels.	The purpose of this model is to maintain a set of accounts on the King's travels.
Accounts receivable.	Manage accounts receivable by recording transactions and printing summary reports.
Expense reports.	This spreadsheet will print the Queen's travel expense reports.

One hallmark of a strong description is a telling verb, an action word that conveys the activity of the model. The right verb animates the description and quickly conveys the model's purpose. The phrase "The purpose of this model is" leaves no question in the reader's mind about the model's goal.

Weak	Strong
Add all the tasks' means and variances and compute the project's mean and variance.	Estimate the length of a project that consists of several tasks.
	Add all the tasks' means and variances and compute the project's mean and variance.

First describe the goal, then how to achieve it. Only if the reader wants to estimate a project's length is he or she interested in the method. The weak version would make a good second line in the strong version. Answer "What?" before "How?" Be sure everyone has agreed on the mountain before you set out to climb it.

Strong

SMALLNEW   17 July 1386   Mother Goose

Provide a framework with which to begin building models.

To use: call it up, change its name, save it with its new name, and edit to your purpose.

Initial Data:	
	Goes here

Model	
	Goes here

Here you see a model devoid of content, yet with a description that serves a purpose. The description succinctly tells what SMALLNEW's purpose is: to provide a framework with which to begin building models. This is a start-up model that you can use to make other models. This simple template saves your having to think about how to organize your work. It allows you to begin by *editing* rather than *writing*.

4. Give clear instructions.

Just as the initial description bridges the gap between the model and the outside world, clear instructions can bridge the gap between the reader of the model and the user of the model. Some who work with a model will only read a paper copy. Others will see it in operation on a computer screen. The description may satisfy the reader, but often the user needs instructions. A step-by-step, numbered list is an excellent way to give clear instructions.

Weak

Directions. Correct the status of the sheep. Group all the lost sheep together. Revise the COUNT and SUM functions in the model. Call up the pie chart entitled SHEEP'S PIE.

Strong

Directions:

1. Correct the "lost" and "found" status of the sheep in the initial data.
2. Sort the initial data to group all the lost sheep together.
3. Revise the COUNT functions under "Number" in the model to count the two groups of lost and found.
4. Revise the SUM functions under "Value" in the model to sum the value of the two groups of lost and found.
5. Call up pie chart entitled SHEEP'S PIE.

The weak and strong examples differ in two important aspects. The obvious aspect is that the strong version is a numbered list. The numbers explicitly order the steps and make it easy for a user to check off each step as it is completed. The subtle aspect is that the weak version is not as clear as it should be. The weak version is a first draft. After you write instructions, be sure to let someone else try to follow them. Such a trial will show you whether the directions are adequate and, if not, how they can be improved. The strong version is a revised draft that was written after readers had trouble following the weak version.

Here is another set of directions (taken completely out of context):

Strong

Directions:
In the initial assumptions area:
1. State the decision and the desired result.
2. Put in choices and make comments.
3. Enter "must" objectives—things that must be satisfied.
4. Enter "want" objectives—things that you would like to have.
5. Weight the importance of the "want" objectives and comment.
6. Rate or rank the choices against each objectives.
> For example, rate the best choice (of four) as 4 and let the others have 3, 2, or 1. You may have ties if you wish. You may rate a choice 0 if you wish.

In the decision model:
7. Examine the model's results and graph.
8. Revise and reexamine the importance of objectives, the rank of choices, and other features to be sure of your choice.
9. List the adverse consequences of the best choice to see if it will work.

Notice that these instructions can stand by themselves. Even without their model they make a certain amount of sense. They are broken into pieces that make it easier for the user to locate where to do which steps. The directions are further clarified in the actual model by a working example which illustrates where within the area to do each step.

A long list of instructions raises the question of where to place it. Frequently, just before the initial data area is a convenient spot. Sometimes, however, the user's needs are best served by including instructions nearer the point where they will be used. In a large model with many pieces, this means that the directions will be moved from the top of the model out to the part of the model where the user will be working. (See discusion of submodels in Chapter 4.) If significant instructions have been moved, leave a note to that effect in the description at the top.

Strong

Instructions on how to use the Monte Carlo portion of the model appear there.

The user can quickly see that the additional support will be available on the Monte Carlo method near its use in the model.

Beyond instructions for the user, more detailed explanations of the ideas behind the model are sometimes necessary to ensure a full understanding of the extent and limitations of the model.

5. Reference critical ideas.

Make a strong reference. Provide a full, accurate guide to the journal, book, or professional communication where the idea originated. Santayana cautioned: "Those who cannot remember the past are condemned to repeat it." Many ideas in a model are original and some borrowed ideas are too simple to bear mention, but an important idea should reveal its past. If it is incorrect, the reader must be given a chance to discover the source of the error. Sometimes an enterprising reader will spot an idea, follow the reference back to the source, and work forward to compose a model tailored to his or her special needs. Do not deny the reader this link to the past.

Strong

Reference: *The Real Mother Goose*. Chicago, IL: Rand McNally, 1916.

Reference: Thomas, Katherine Elwes. *The Real Personages of Mother Goose*. Boston, MA: Lonthrop, Lee & Shepard Co., 1930.

Reference: Kepner, Charles H., and Tregoe, Benjamin B. *The New Rational Manager*. Princeton, NJ: Princeton Research Press, 1981.

Reference: Nevison, John M. *The Little Book of BASIC Style: How to Write a Program You Can Read*. Reading, MA: Addison-Wesley, 1978.

Reference: See Materials Handling Procedure Manual, Document Number A34.77, Rev. 3.6, pp. 64–68.

Reference: If you have any questions, call Bo Peep at extension 3456.

A reference need not be only to a book. A knowledgeable individual, a file with related information, a standard form the organization has been using for years; each can be an appropriate reference in certain circumstances.

6. Map the contents.

The underlying organization of a spreadsheet is spatial. Geography is all. To let the user know where things are requires a map. One of the most convenient maps is a table of contents. If the sections of your model are kept to the left and stacked vertically, the table of contents can be an accurate map to the location of each part of the model.

A table of contents is the last part of the introduction in all but the smallest spreadsheets. As soon as a spreadsheet slips off the screen and escapes your visual span of control, you will need a table of contents to see where you are.

Strong

Ninepence   10 December 1536   King Henry

To show how income is distributed in the kingdom

Contents:
>   Introduction: Title, description, contents.
>   Initial data and beginning assumptions
>   Income distribution model
>   Report on kingdom's spending for the year
>   Report on distribution of royal burden
>   Data for pie chart of burden

A table of contents is a powerful organizer for a reader. If the reader is only concerned with the spending report, he or she can focus her attention on it at once. If the reader wishes to know more about the data that led to the graphs, he or she knows where to look.

The name in the table of contents should correspond to the name in that area of the spreadsheet. If named ranges are available, you should name the areas of the spreadsheet and display those names in the table of contents to keep them visible.

Strong

Tenpence   10 December 1536   King Henry

To show how income is distributed in the kingdom

Contents: (each section is a named range)
 INTRO   Introduction: Title, description, contents.
 INITIAL   Initial data and beginning assumptions
 MODEL   Income distribution model
 REPORT1   Report on kingdom's spending for the year
 REPORT2   Report on distribution of royal burden
 GRAPH   Data for pie chart of burden

Here the named range is on the left and a larger explanation appears on the right. Tenpence gives the user an extra reason to be interested in the table of contents: by using the named ranges the user can jump to the right place in the spreadsheet. Named ranges also avoid the annoying problem of using cell locations that must be changed every time the spreadsheet is rearranged. The reader of a printed version of the model welcomes the extra information about the organization of the spreadsheet.

Strong

NEW   17 July 1386   Mother Goose
(C) Copyright 1985 by John M. Nevison

Provide a framework with which to begin building models.

To use: call it up, change its name, save it with its new name, and edit to your purpose.

Contents: (each section is a named range)
 INTRO   Introduction: Title, description, contents, and map.
 INITIAL   Initial data and beginning assumptions
 MODEL   Model
 OTHERS   Other sections as necessary

Initial data and beginning assumptions
                         Go here

Model
                     Goes here

This template, NEW, extends the template SMALLNEW by including a table of contents. NEW is the common starting place for most of the spreadsheets in this book. The already named ranges give the user a head start with the work.

Sometimes a model's geography has horizontal spread as well as vertical depth. If so, include a map beneath the table of contents.

Weak	*Strong*		
Contents	Contents		
North America	North America		
Europe	Europe		
Asia	Asia		
South America	South America		
Africa	Africa		
Australia	Australia		
Antarctica	Antarctica		
	Map		
	North America	Europe	Asia
	South America	Africa	
			Australia
	Antarctica		

Weak	*Strong*	
Contents	Contents	
raw material purchases	raw material purchases	
payables	payables	
finished product orders	finished product orders	
receivables	receivables	
general ledger	general ledger	
payroll	payroll	
	Map	
	raw material purchases	finished product orders
	payables	receivable
	general ledger	
	payroll	

With the continents mapped, the user knows which way to travel with his cursor, the reader knows which way to travel with his eye. The reader knows when to go down and when to go sideways. The raw materials and finished products are arranged in parallel. They feed the general ledger which is below them. The payroll is a separate function below the general ledger.

The map tells the user where he can safely insert rows and columns. The Australia section can have rows inserted in it without hitting Africa. The user knows at once where the lower right corner of the model is: below Antarctica and to the right of Australia, below payroll and to the right of receivable.

Experienced users testify that a map is a powerful way to reclaim control over a spreadsheet that has gotten out of hand. The map organizes and informs. Sometimes it will even point out how to reorganize your model. It will always make your model easier to comprehend, to grasp as a whole. A map restores your visual span of control over even the largest spreadsheets.

Beyond a sharp title, a clear purpose, good directions, helpful references, and a simple map, your introduction may include additional information. What you should add to the description depends on the function of the model, the knowledge of the reader, the skill of the user, and the framework of the organization within which the model will be used. (See Chapter 6 for more discussion of the organization.) Err on the side of overinforming your reader. He may not be stupid, but he is probably more ignorant than you suspect. Your introduction should include everything necessary to make a successful bridge from the model itself to the world in which it will be used.

After the spreadsheet has been thoroughly introduced, it must set to work to achieve its purpose. Good spreadsheet form is more architecture than interior design. The next rules define the second and third parts, the major architectural elements, of the basic form: the Initial Data Area and the Model Area. The spreadsheet's goal is to arrive clearly at the desired results. Each part serves this goal in its own way. The Initial Data Area stores the beginning material of the model, the raw data and the initial assumptions. The Model Area is where formulas manufacture consequences from the raw material. Here complex formulas are explained, intermediate terms appear, and final results are often displayed.

THE INITIAL DATA AREA

7. Identify the data.

Data are the grist for the model's mill. They are numbers you know when you write the model. They may be three key constants or 3,000 items in a database. They belong in their own area where they may be clearly labeled and conveniently arranged. Such an area makes it easy for both reader and user to identify the data.

Without an Initial Data Area a weak model can be an unintended mystery.

Weak

INFLATE A   1 January 1510   J. Horner
(C) Copyright 1983 John M. Nevison

Find the profit margin in an inflationary world where raw material costs, labor costs, and prices each grow at a different rate.

Growth Rate		1.03	1.15		1.07		
	Year	Raw mat	Labor	Total cst	Price	Profit	Margin
	1510	56.00	21.00	77.00	100.00	23.00	23.00%
	1511	57.68	24.15	81.83	107.00	25.17	23.52%
	1512	59.41	27.77	87.18	114.49	27.31	23.85%
	1513	61.19	31.94	93.13	122.50	29.37	23.98%
	1514	63.03	36.73	99.76	131.08	31.32	23.90%
	1515	64.92	42.24	107.16	140.26	33.10	23.60%

This weak example does not have an Initial Data Area. It is more puzzle than model. The model shows the profit of a product with different cost components growing at different rates. You see that a price increase of 7%—a 7% increase has a factor of 1.07—preserves profit margin. But you don't know with any certainty what the initial data are.

Strong

INFLATE B   1 January 1510   J. Horner
(C) Copyright 1984 by John M. Nevison

Test pricing in an inflationary world where different costs growing
at different rates affect the margin (% profit). By varying the
price growth rate the user can attempt to preserve a certain
margin in some future year.

Contents: (each section is a named range)
INTRO   Introductory material: Title, description, and contents.
INIT   Initial data
MODEL   Model

Initial Data:
                  1510   Starting Year

Cost structure		Growth rates	
$56.00	Raw material cost	1.03	Raw material growth rate
$21.00	Labor cost	1.15	Labor growth rate
$100.00	Price	1.07	Price growth rate

Model

YEAR	MATERIAL	LABOR	TOTLCOST	PRICE	PROFIT	MARGIN
1510	56.00	21.00	77.00	100.00	23.00	23.00%
1511	57.68	24.15	81.83	107.00	25.17	23.52%
1512	59.41	27.77	87.18	114.49	27.31	23.85%
1513	61.19	31.94	93.13	122.50	29.37	23.98%
1514	63.03	36.73	99.76	131.08	31.32	23.90%
1515	64.92	42.24	107.16	140.26	33.10	23.60%

In the strong example the Initial Data Area lets you see what's going on. The
starting year, the assumptions about the cost structure of the product, and the
growth factors are all clearly identified.

Not only can you use the initial model quicker, you can modify it faster. (Suppose the user had a different product with an $83.00 price, a $40.00 cost of labor, and a $10.00 raw material cost.)

Aristotle once observed: "Well begun is half done." The Initial Data Area sketches out the scope of the model before you actually encounter the Model Area. When you have seen the initial values, you can guess at the information to be derived from them. By knowing which terms are the independent assumptions, you have a good idea how the model may be manipulated to achieve a variety of answers.

Storing the data in a separate Initial Data Area makes it easier to ask the "what if" questions that depend on varying the initial data. You can also update a whole set of initial data without getting ensnarled in the thicket of formulas in the Model Area. Keeping the data separate from the model lowers the chance that you will accidentally alter a formula.

Strong

ACTIVITY TRACK   3 January 1520   T. Tittlemouse
(C) Copyright 1985 by John M. Nevison

Track the number of assigned activities during a project.
The project is to build a new catapult.

To use:
   1. Enter the new weekly data in the Initial Data.
   2. Examine the model
   3. Print the graphs.

Contents: (each section is a named range)
   INTRO   Introduction: Title, description, contents.
   INITIAL Initial data and beginning assumptions
   MODEL   Quarterly model
   GRAPH   Graphing area
   VERIFY   Verify area

Initial data and beginning assumptions

Activities as they occurred

Week number	1	2	3	4	5	6	7	8	9	10	11	12	13	14	15	16	...	52
Design activities																		
Assigned	5	6	7	7	7	8	7	6	6	5	4	4	3	3	3	2	...	0
Completed	0	3	4	5	6	7	7	6	5	4	5	6	5	4	4	4	...	0
Build activities																		
Assigned	0	0	0	0	0	0	3	4	5	4	4	5	6	7	5	6	...	0
Completed	0	0	0	0	0	0	0	2	4	5	4	5	5	6	6	4	...	0
Test activities																		
Assigned	0	0	0	0	0	0	0	0	0	0	0	0	0	0	0	0	...	0
Completed	0	0	0	0	0	0	0	0	0	0	0	0	0	0	0	0	...	0

Quarterly model

THE CATAPULT PROJECT: activities completed in early autumn.

1520

	Qtr 1	Qtr 2	Qtr 3	Qtr 4	Total	
Design activities						Date: 3 January 1521
Assigned	75	11	0	0	86	
Completed	63	23	0	0	86	
Build activities						
Assigned	31	79	14	0	124	
Completed	25	71	28	0	124	
Test activities						
Assigned	0	29	33	1	63	
Completed	0	17	35	11	63	
Total activities						
Assigned	106	119	47	1	273	
Completed	88	111	63	11	273	

You see again how much easier it is to use a model that extricates the raw numbers from the model itself. ACTIVITY TRACK clearly separates raw data from the quarterly model. The user can easily add weekly data without intruding into the Model Area. ACTIVITY TRACK labels the initial data so the reader sees that the data is collected weekly, to be used in a quarterly fashion. (In fact, data this numerous cry out to be graphed, and the full model contains a rather elaborate graphing area to support the spreadsheet's graphs. See Chapter 4 for more details.)

A model with unidentified data can turn the reader into an unwilling detective.

Weak

PLAN A   22 Aug 1485   Humpty Dumpty

Make a five-year income statement projection.
Begin with sales, subtract costs that are a percentage of sales or
are constant, find net income.

Model

	1486	1487	1488	1489	1490
Sales	100.00	108.00	116.64	125.97	136.05
Cost of goods sold	42.50	45.90	49.57	53.54	57.82
Gross profit	57.50	62.10	67.07	72.43	78.23
S G & A	33.00	35.64	38.49	41.57	44.90
Depreciation	7.00	7.00	7.00	7.00	7.00
Fixed expenses	40.00	42.64	45.49	48.57	51.90
Interest	2.25	2.25	2.25	2.25	2.25
Profit before tax	15.25	17.21	19.33	21.61	24.08
Tax	6.10	6.88	7.73	8.65	9.63
Net Income	9.15	10.33	11.60	12.97	14.45

Strong

PLAN B   22 August 1485   Humpty Dumpty

Make a five-year income statement projection.
Begin with sales, subtract costs that are a percentage of sales or are constant, find net income.

Contents: (each section is a named range)
  INTRO   Introduction: Title, description, contents, and map.
  INITIAL Initial data and beginning assumptions
  MODEL   Income statement projection

Initial data and beginning assumptions
1486   Starting year
100.00   Sales for starting year
7.00   Depreciation
2.25   Interest

Income statement projection

	1486	1487	1488	1489	1490
Sales	100.00	108.00	116.64	125.97	136.05
Cost of goods sold	42.50	45.90	49.57	53.54	57.82
Gross profit	57.50	62.10	67.07	72.43	78.23
S G & A	33.00	35.64	38.49	41.57	44.90
Depreciation	7.00	7.00	7.00	7.00	7.00
Fixed expenses	40.00	42.64	45.49	48.57	51.90
Interest	2.25	2.25	2.25	2.25	2.25
Profit before tax	15.25	17.21	19.33	21.61	24.08
Tax	6.10	6.88	7.73	8.65	9.63
Net Income	9.15	10.33	11.60	12.97	14.45

PLAN B tells you more than PLAN A. You, the reader, understand for the first time what the raw data of this model are: the starting year of 1490, the starting sales of $100, the constant $7 depreciation, and the constant $2.25 interest. You feel you have some of the answers to the mystery. Yet for all its improvement over PLAN A, PLAN B is not complete. The witness is still holding back: the spreadsheet still hides assumptions from the reader.

8. Surface and label every assumption.

One of the most serious errors of spreadsheet modeling is burying an assumption. A raw number—a constant, a factor, or a rate—can lurk submerged in a formula in the model. Such an assumption must be forced to the surface and clearly labeled. It should be placed *before* the model in the Initial Data Area.

Surfacing an assumption gives you an opportunity to label it. This label can go a long way towards explaining the true nature of the model.

Strong

PLAN C   22 August 1485   Humpty Dumpty

Make a five-year income statement projection.
Begin with sales, subtract costs that are a percentage of sales or are
constant, find net income.

Contents: (each section is a named range)
 INTRO   Introduction: Title, description, contents, and map.
 INITIAL Initial data and beginning assumptions
 MODEL   Income statement projection

Initial data and beginning assumptions

	1486	Starting year			
	100.00	Sales for starting year			
	8.0%	Annual sales growth rate			
	42.5%	Cost of goods sold as a percentage of sales			
	33.0%	Selling, general, and administrative costs as a percentage of sales			
	15.0%	Interest rate			
	40.0%	Tax rate			
	1486	1487	1488	1489	1490
Depreciation	7.00	7.00	7.00	7.00	7.00
Debt	15.00	15.00	15.00	15.00	15.00

Income statement projection

	1486	1487	1488	1489	1490
Sales	100.00	108.00	116.64	125.97	136.05
Cost of goods sold	42.50	45.90	49.57	53.54	57.82
Gross profit	57.50	62.10	67.07	72.43	78.23
S G & A	33.00	35.64	38.49	41.57	44.90
Depreciation	7.00	7.00	7.00	7.00	7.00
Fixed expenses	40.00	42.64	45.49	48.57	51.90
Interest	2.25	2.25	2.25	2.25	2.25
Profit before tax	15.25	17.21	19.33	21.61	24.08
Tax	6.10	6.88	7.73	8.65	9.63
Net Income	9.15	10.33	11.60	12.97	14.45

Finally you see the hidden details of PLAN. The buried assumptions are: the 8% annual growth rate, the 42.5% cost of goods sold as a percentage of sales, the 33% selling, general, and administrative costs as a percentage of sales, the 15% interest rate, and the 40% tax rate. You also see that depreciation and debt are assumed to be constant over the five-year period. Because the constants are spread out in the initial data, the reader can infer that the author thought it likely that the user might want to change a value in any year.

Sometimes a spreadsheet identifies the data but combines the Initial Data Area with another area. This possibility is explored later in this chapter in the section entitled "Using the Basic Form."

THE MODEL AREA

9. Model to explain.

A model is a web of relations woven with formulas. If you have assiduously separated out raw data and initial assumptions, then the model itself should be pure formulas.

The formulas of the model are themselves assumptions. The first responsibility of the Model Area is to explain clearly what assumptions are embedded in the formulas. The Model Area should provide three levels of explanation:

- the values that appear in the model,
- the written explanation of any tricky formulas, and
- the complete printout of all the formulas in the model.

The Model Area's first level of explanation is the values that appear in the cells. If a formula produces results that are not entirely clear, it is a good idea to break the formula into its component pieces, where each step can be viewed.

Weak	Strong
1402.08 :Total expense	1402.08 :Total expense
674.08 :Total adjustment	250.00 :Cash advance
	478.00 :Other prepaid
	674.08 :Total adjustment

Here you see how the total travel expenses were reduced by cash advances and prepaid charges (such as conference registrations) to arrive at the total adjustment. In the weak example, the intermediate numbers are hidden in a formula; in the strong they are presented as intermediate results.

How much to explain depends on the reader's and user's backgrounds. When you are in doubt, err on the side of overexplaining. Six months later, oversimplified steps will be a welcome relief as you struggle to read your own model. If someone else uses the model, the steps will increase his or her confidence in its accuracy.

A formula should be easy to read aloud. If a formula gets so complicated that it is hard to read aloud, it probably should be broken into two formulas. If you break the formula into pieces and the intermediate values in the extra cells intrude on the layout of the report you were preparing, create a separate region below the model for making the report.

The Model Area's second level of explanation is a written summary of all tricky formulas. For example, the model below changes the independent variable from sales to net income. As a result, the Model Area must explain some tricky formulas.

Strong

PLAN D   22 August 1485   Humpty Dumpty
   22 February 1486   Tom Tucker

Make a five-year income statement projection based on net income growth. Begin with net income, add costs that are a percentage of net income or are constant, find sales.

Contents: (each section is a named range)
INTRO   Introduction: Title, description, contents, and map.
INITIAL   Initial data and beginning assumptions
MODEL   Income statement projection

Initial data and beginning assumptions

1486	Starting year
9.15	Net income starting year
10.0%	Annual net income growth rate
464.5%	Cost of goods sold as a percentage of net income
360.7%	Selling, general and administrative costs as a percentage of net income
15.0%	Interest rate
40.0%	Tax rate

	1486	1487	1488	1489	1490
Depreciation	7.00	7.00	7.00	7.00	7.00
Debt	15.00	15.00	15.00	15.00	15.00

Income statement projection

Tricky formulas below include:
> Tax from net = (net/(1-tax rate))*tax rate
> SG&A = (SG&A %)*Net
> Cost of goods sold = (COGS %)*net

	1486	1487	1488	1489	1490
Net Income	9.15	10.06	11.07	12.18	13.40
Tax	6.10	6.71	7.38	8.12	8.93
Profit before tax	15.25	16.77	18.45	20.30	22.33
Interest	2.25	2.25	2.25	2.25	2.25
S G & A	33.00	36.30	39.93	43.92	48.32
Depreciation	15.00	15.00	15.00	15.00	15.00
Fixed expenses	48.00	51.30	54.93	58.92	63.32
Cost of goods sold	42.50	46.75	51.43	56.57	62.22
Gross profit	33.00	36.30	39.93	43.92	48.32
Sales	75.50	83.05	91.36	100.49	110.54

You need help with the formulas in this model because PLAN D turns PLAN C on its head. PLAN C began with sales and ended with net income; PLAN D does the reverse. In the inverted model, a few formulas get tricky and they have been explained near where they occur. PLAN D also reverses the order of the lines in the model to make the top-to-bottom flow of the reader correspond to the top-to-bottom flow of the calculation. The Model Area is trying above all to show how the calculations are performed. In order to get an easy-to-read report, a Report Area can be added (see Chapter 4 for details).

The Model Area's third level of explanation of the calculations is a printed copy of all the formulas in the model. In the case of PLAN D it might look like this:

First three years of model (detail):

	1490	1491	1492
Net Income	9.15	10.06	11.07
Tax	6.10	6.71	7.38
Profit before tax	15.25	16.77	18.45
Interest	2.25	2.25	2.25
S G & A	33.00	36.30	39.93
Depreciation	15.00	15.00	15.00
Fixed expenses	48.00	51.30	54.93
Cost of goods sold	42.50	46.75	51.43
Gross profit	33.00	36.30	39.93
Sales	75.50	83.05	91.36

First three years of model as formulas (detail):

	$=B14$	$=C33+1$	$=D33+1$
"Net Income	$=\$B\$15$ fix 2	$=C35*(1+\$B\$16)$ fix 2	$=D35*(1+\$B\$16)$ fix 2
"Tax	$=C35/(1-\$B\$21)*\$B21$ fix 2 p	$=D35/(1-\$B\$21)*\$B21$ fix 2 p	$=E35/(1-\$B\$21)*\$B21$ fix 2 p
"Profit before tax	$=C35+C36$ fix 2	$=D35+D36$ fix 2	$=E35+E36$ fix 2

"Interest	= $B$20*C24 fix 2	= $B$20*D24 fix 2	= $B$20*E24 fix 2
"S G & A	= $B$18*C35 fix 2	= $B$18*D35 fix 2	= $B$18*E35 fix 2
"Depreciation	= C24 fix 2	= D24 fix 2	= E24 fix 2
"Fixed expenses	= C40 + C41 fix 2	= D40 + D41 fix 2	= E40 + E41 fix 2
"Cost of goods sold	= $B$17*C35 fix 2	= $B$17*D35 fix 2	= $B$17*E35 fix 2
"Gross profit	= C38 + C40 + C43 fix 2	= D38 + D40 + D43 fix 2	= E38 + E40 + E43 fix 2
"Sales	= C45 + C44 fix 2	= D45 + D44 fix 2	= E45 + E44 fix 2

Be sure when you print a paper copy of the finished model for the reader that you print a second version with the model's formulas. (See Chapter 6 for more on this idea.) Details on how to print formulas are given in the appendixes.

Formulas may well appear in other parts of the spreadsheet besides the Model Area. One frequent use of a formula in the Initial Data Area is to make sure that one piece of data implies another. For example, if you wish to divide something between two players using a percentage, the results might look like this:

Weak	Strong (formula)	Strong (values)
.14 Player A .86 Player B	.14 Player A (1 − $A$5) Player B where .14 is in cell A5	14% Player A 86% Player B

The strong version uses a formula to avoid an entry error. One entry gets two correct results.

Formulas may occur in other regions as well. Wherever a formula appears, its function should be apparent, and should support the particular area's purpose (see Chapter 4 for more on other areas).

10. Point to the right source.

As you build your formulas you will have occasion to refer to an earlier cell for a value. Whenever you do this, be sure you are referring to the right occurrence of the value. That is, be sure you point to the value that makes it easiest for the reader and user to understand the formula. If the best source is another cell in the body of the model, it will be nearby and will have the context of the model to help explain it. If the best source is in the initial data, it will probably have some explanatory text near it. The right source is the one that speeds the reader's comprehension of the formula.

For example, consider the following three lines from the body of the model in Plan C.

Strong

		A	B	C	D
31	S G & A			+$B$17*C27	+$B$17*D27
32	Depreciation			+C22	+D22
33	Fixed expenses			+C31+C32	+D31+D32

The formula for selling, general, and administrative costs (S G & A) uses the fixed percentage found in the initial area at $B$17. Initial data items that appear as single values often get used as "absolute" cells in model formulas. In this case, pointing to the original source is the method that best illustrates what the formula means.

In line 33, however, you see a different solution to the problem. The good formula C33 = +C31+C32 says "add the two lines above." Fixed expenses equals S G &A plus depreciation. Any other form would make more work for the reader. The poor alternative C33 = +C31 +C22 embroils the reader in an unnecessary search for what's going on up in row 22.

When a line, column, or row of initial data—such as Depreciation—is included in a formula, usually the best course is to refer to the nearby line in the model. The line has been included in the model to make it easier to read, and it usually follows that it is the better choice when building nearby lines in the body of the model.

An isolated single value, however, is almost always better referred to the original source. If you make it a habit to refer to the original source, the reader of the paper version can make sense out of the model more quickly, and the user of the model can handle the model with greater certainty. Both know that if they change the model in the initial data area, they are changing the unique reference point that feeds formulas all over the model.

THE DUAL ROLE OF THE MODEL AREA

In the basic form the Model Area plays two roles—as the area that explains the calculations and as the area that displays the results. Because many spreadsheets can be built with the Model Area also serving the purpose of the Report Area, discussion of the Report Area is deferred to Chapter 4. If a conflict arises between being clear about the calculation and displaying the results, a Report Area should be added.

The basic form is the essential first step of good spreadsheet design. The Introduction, the Initial Data Area, and the Model Area form a powerful triumvirate, the fundamental triad of a good design. The ten basic rules in this chapter will help you build models that can be used and reused with confidence.

USING THE BASIC FORM

Even with discussion of the Report Area deferred, serious questions remain about the relationship between the Initial Data Area and the Model Area. At first, the idea of a separate Initial Data Area may appear to violate the fundamental simplicity of spreadsheets. But remember that the rule is not "Set up an Initial Data Area," the rule is "Identify the data."

The mystery spreadsheet below focuses the issue. What do you call it?

Mystery spreadsheet

	Column of row sums
Mass of raw	.
numbers in	.
a large table.	.
Row of column sums . . .	Grand total

Is this an Initial Data Area with a few extra formulas? A Model Area without an Initial Data Area? Or a Report Area without an Initial Data Area or a Model Area?

To answer these questions, remind yourself that the Initial Data Area identifies the raw data, the Model Area explains the calculations, and the Report Area prints the results for a particular reader. If you can make one area display the raw data, explain the calculation, and print out clear results, then call it an Initial Data Area. The first requirement is the greatest requirement: you must always identify the data.

If the mystery spreadsheet is an Initial Data Area with a few added formulas, and if you add more formulas to the first few, at what point should the spreadsheet spawn a Model Area?

First form

Initial Data Area

	Column of row sums
Mass of raw	.
INTERMEDIATE ROW OF FORMULAS	.
numbers in	.
INTERMEDIATE ROW OF FORMULAS	.
a large table.	.
Row of column sums . . .	Grand total

When should you split this into two areas? When you become uncomfortable thinking that identifying the data is the primary purpose of the spreadsheet. When the calculations become confused or obscure. When you need room to rearrange the model to make it easier to read. Any one of these reasons is sufficient cause for a Model Area.

Second form

Initial Data Area

Mass of raw

    numbers in

        a large table

           (with explanations.)

Model Area

	Column of row sums
Mass of raw	.
INTERMEDIATE ROW OF FORMULAS	.
numbers in	.
INTERMEDIATE ROW OF FORMULAS	.
a large table.	.
Row of column sums . . .	Grand total

When you break the spreadsheet into two areas, you may be bothered by seeing a big block of numbers twice, but you will find compensatory freedoms. You will be able to label the initial data clearly without intruding on your model's format. You will also be able to shape the model to reveal what the calculations are and to convince the reader that these calculations are correct.

If separating the Initial Data Area and the Model Area makes you feel stupid at first, do it anyway. If, after a few months of going out of your way to apply these rules, your models are not substantially better, back off from this practice until you find a balance that is right for you and for the users of your spreadsheets. Your overriding concern should be for ease of use over ease of construction, for clarity of expression over speed of writing.

A WORD ON BUILDING THE INITIAL DATA AREA
AND THE MODEL AREA

When writing a new model, one way to develop the initial data is by beginning with a template like NEW and building the Model Area first. When you write a formula with a constant in it (for example, King Henry's 23% tax rate in Chapter 1), you can stop, write and label the assumption up in the Initial Data Area, return to the model, and rewrite the formula with a reference to the Initial Data Area. So the old formula may have looked like this:

B30 = A30*.23

while the new formula looks like this:

B30 = A30*$B$5

and B5 and B6 look like this:

23% Tax rate

As you continue building the model you may find a row or column of raw numbers. Again, you move the raw numbers up to the Initial Data Area and change the model entry to a one-term formula that refers to the raw data. You will have changed the old model:

B36 = 18,346

to the new model:

B36 = +B15

where the new initial data is:

B15 = 18,346.

The result of these efforts will be a Model Area that is *entirely formulas*. Such efforts will force you to think about the spreadsheet's use while the spreadsheet model is being built. The final spreadsheet will benefit from this extra thought.

SPREADSHEETS THAT DO NOT HAVE MODEL AREAS

Some spreadsheets are exceptions to the basic rules. Rules should aid your common sense, not replace it. Some spreadsheets honestly do not need a Model Area. Here's one example:

Strong

TRAVEL   15 June 1588   Queen Elizabeth

Print the Queen's travel expenses.
To use:
1. Call up program and save with a new name.
2. Enter trip information in the appropriate places.
3. Collect all the prepaid expenses as a formula in the "prepaid expenses" cell.
4. Include appropriate notes.
5. Print a copy for your personal records and a copy for the Treasury.

Initial data, beginning assumptions, and travel report.

TRAVEL EXPENSES OF QUEEN ELIZABETH

Date: 23-28 September 1588   Purpose: To talk with the lords and visit
Name: Queen Elizabeth   the people.
Trip: Visit to Banbury Cross

	SUN	MON	TUE	WED	THR	FRI	SAT	TOTAL
Travel		96.00	96.00	110.00	80.00	96.00		478.00
Local trans								0.00
Stable		24.00	32.00	38.00	44.00	23.00		161.00
Inn	104.85	97.97	103.77	100.42	95.57			502.58
Meals								0.00
Breakfast		8.00	8.00		35.00	5.00		56.00
Lunch			5.00		5.00	45.00		55.00
Dinner	15.50	25.00	45.00	27.00		10.00		122.50
Entertainment		3.00	4.00	2.00	4.00	3.00		16.00
Miscellaneous		3.00		8.00				11.00
Total	120.35	256.97	293.77	285.42	263.57	182.00	0.00	1,402.08

1402.08 :Total expense   Signed: _____
 250.00 :Treasury advance
 478.00 :Other (prepaid)   Date: _____
 674.08 :Total adjustment

   0.00 :Due treasury
 674.08 :Due Queen

Notes: Tue. dinner with mayor.
        Thursday B'fast with castle force,
        Fri. lunch with General.

TRAVEL is a spreadsheet that does not need a Model Area. It has only a very few simple equations. Its purpose is to identify the initial data and present it clearly, so the author calls it an Initial Data Area with a few totals. We do not have a Model Area at all. What we print out is the Initial Data Area.

Databases are another case where the Initial Data Area overwhelms the Model Area. (Often, however, databases trail summary reports that are Model Areas.)

Strong

SHEEP   15 April 1566   Bo Peep

Maintain a database on the sheep herd. Track the number and value of the lost and found sheep. Revise it periodically to keep it current.

WARNING: This model will be incorrect between the time the data is re-sorted and the model's functions are revised. (See directions for details.)

Contents: (each section is a named range)
INTRO   Introduction: Title, description, contents and directions.
INITIAL Initial data and beginning assumptions
MODEL   Sheep count model
GRAPH   Sheep pie chart data

Directions:

1. Correct the "lost" and "found" status of the sheep in the initial data.
2. Sort the initial data to group all the lost sheep together.
3. Revise the COUNT functions under "Number" in the model to count the two groups of lost and found.
4. Revise the SUM functions under "Value" in the model to sum the value of the two groups of lost and found.
5. Call up pie chart entitled SHEEP'S PIE.

Initial data and beginning assumptions

NAME	STATUS	COLOR	VALUE
Brian	Found	White	100
Ian	Found	White	200
Margaret	Found	Plaid	200
Angus	Found	Black	300
Janet	Lost	White	400
Hugh	Lost	Red	300
Alistair	Lost	White	100
Mary	Lost	White	100
Agnes	Lost	White	200

Sheep count model

	Number	Percent	Value
Lost	5	56%	1100
Found	4	44%	800
Total	9	100%	1900

Sheep pie chart data

	Value	Percent value
Lost	1100	58%
Found	800	42%

VALUE OF LOST SHEEP

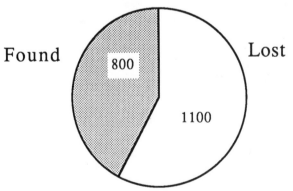

SHEEP is a collection of data with a modest model wagging along behind. There are no major assumptions, just a collection of data. Notice that the model has spun off a graphics area (more on that in Chapter 4). A major reason for dividing a spreadsheet into areas is that it makes later modification easier.

With a very large database you might want to rearrange the contents to have two different areas for data: an area for the "what if" initial assumptions, and a database for the bulk of the raw data.

Data in a database may be so large and may change so often that you want to keep them below the rest of the model. This practice has the advantage that the location of your reports remains stable, since it is above the insertion and deletion of rows that constantly vary the size of the database. If the sheep herd had numbered in the hundreds, Bo Peep might have structured the model like this:

Strong

Contents:	(each section is a named range)
INTRO	Introduction: Title, description, contents and directions.
INITIAL	Initial data and beginning assumptions
MODEL	Sheep count model
GRAPH	Sheep pie chart data
DATA	Database of sheep data

3

THE MIND'S EYE: DESIGN

MULTIPLICATION IS VEXATION

Multiplication is vexation,
Division is as bad;
The Rule of Three doth puzzle me,
And Practice drives me mad.

The problem of design includes working out ideas in advance and testing completed structures. Design also encompasses an abiding concern for the overall appearance of things. The next four procedural rules help you apply the first ten. They suggest what to do and when: they are rules for the mind's eye.

11. First design on paper.

Do your first thinking with pencil and paper. Design can encompass many things, but one thing is certain: your first idea will not be your last and only rarely will it be your best. Ideas demand editing. You will need to react to your initial impulse, to brood over your vision, to rearrange, to revise, to rethink. All of this is much easier done on paper. If you resist the intemperate urge to type on the computer and instead deliberate over your initial design on paper, you will complete your whole project faster.

If you cannot resist the urge to leap to your computer and begin typing, please think of your first efforts as being "paper" efforts. Use nonsense collections of letters such as "xxx yyy xxx" to simulate text, and rows or columns of 99999.99 to simulate quickly what a block of numbers will look like. Move blocks of your spreadsheets around until you have a good feel for the gross arrangement of the whole model. In short, tell yourself that your first efforts are to sketch a preliminary design and to mull over basic ideas.

When beginning an absolutely new model, some find it helpful to write a one-sentence statement of purpose that begins, "The purpose of this spreadsheet is. . . ." This sentence can be followed by a paragraph that begins, "How the spreadsheet achieves this purpose is. . . ." For people who think best with words, these two phrases can cut a clear path through a lot of fuzzy thinking.

For those who prefer pictures, sketches on a large piece of paper can be a big help. You can lay out each region as a block. Within a region, columns and rows can appear as subblocks. Areas for text can be outlined to see how the general shape and size will appear. The blocks can be arranged so that they relate to each other in the best way. Blocks that create information can be placed ahead of blocks that use that information.

Your model will be easier to read if you group areas that work together. A tricky formula is easier to explore if its constituent elements lie nearby. Grouping allows nearby references to be quickly checked.

Design from the major idea to the minor. Start with the area of central importance—the model or the database—and work out to the minor regions—back to the initial data and description, forward to submodels that compute pieces of data, over to collateral models that develop parallel figures. Sometimes the area of central importance will be a report, sometimes a graph.

Don't be surprised if the region of central importance shifts. Sometimes you may begin thinking your model's report is the central idea, only to discover that the real heart of the matter is a graph. Stay clear in your own mind about what the major idea is. This clarity of purpose will allow you to design faster and better.

If your current idea is not a totally new one, sometimes an old design can serve as a template for your new project. By using a template you are less likely to overlook a necessary part and more likely to cast your final ideas in a form familiar to your eye. Be sure that you don't let the old idea unnecessarily restrict you. Be prepared to break the mold and move on to a new and better approach if your idea requires it.

If you have been doing your initial "paper" design on the computer, remember that you can systematically extract regions from the rough draft and move them to a brand new spreadsheet (or insert them into a preexisting template). Extracting a few good regions is sometimes faster than editing many bad ones. However, when you extract, you will lose special definitions of column width and special formats for cells.

Design your spreadsheet once so that it can be used many times. One hard test for a good design is ease of reuse. If a model is easy to reuse, it is probably designed in a straightforward manner. If you think about how the model could be used a year from now, you will probably design it better. Design it to last five years.

12. Test and edit.

A correct model requires testing, just as clear English requires editing. As you work on your model in solitude, you should do both: test your spreadsheet by varying the initial parameters and seeing if the appropriate conclusions are altered in the expected ways; edit your comments to make sure they stay current with the model as you build and revise it.

You may more fully test a model by using a known example to be sure the answer agrees with the known correct answer. You may use 0's and 1's for a quick practice, but you should avoid them when providing sample data to verify formally that the final model is correct.

Weak

Model
Tricky formulas:
  Expected = (low + 4*likely + high)/6
  Standard deviation = (high − low)/6
  Variance = (standard deviation)^2
  Project standard deviation = square root(project variance)

Task name	Low	Likely	High	Expected	Variance	
Activity 1	0	3	6	3.0	1.0	
Activity 2	0	3	6	3.0	1.0	
Activity 3	0	3	6	3.0	1.0	
Activity 4	0	3	6	3.0	1.0	
Activity 5	0	3	6	3.0	1.0	
Activity 6	0	3	6	3.0	1.0	
Activity 7	0	3	6	3.0	1.0	
Activity 8	0	3	6	3.0	1.0	
						Standard deviation
Project totals				24.0	8.0	2.8
Check sums	0	24	48	24.0		

Strong

Model
Tricky formulas:
 Expected = (low + 4*likely + high)/6
 Standard deviation = (high − low)/6
 Variance = (standard deviation)^2
 Project standard deviation = square root(project variance)

Task name	Low	Likely	High	Expected	Variance	
Activity 1	2	5	14	6.0	4.0	
Activity 2	2	5	14	6.0	4.0	
Activity 3	2	5	14	6.0	4.0	
Activity 4	2	5	14	6.0	4.0	
Activity 5	2	5	14	6.0	4.0	
Activity 6	2	5	14	6.0	4.0	
Activity 7	2	5	14	6.0	4.0	
Activity 8	2	5	14	6.0	4.0	
						Standard deviation
Project totals				54.0	36.0	6.0
Check sums	18	45	126	54.0		

The test data should try to avoid 0's and 1's because they do special things that might mask errors. For example, 1^2 is 1 while 2^2 is 4. If there were a mistake in squaring the standard deviation to compute the variance, it would not be visible if the standard deviation was 1. Zero added to anything, or one multiplied by anything, does not change it. In test data, use numbers that change things.

A strong set of test data can be checked by hand. This model has four tricky equations that can be verified by inspection when a strong set of initial data is applied. The numbers 2 and 14 are the smallest positive whole numbers (larger than one) that yield a standard deviation that is a whole number bigger than 1. Five is the smallest whole number between 2 and 14 that yields a whole number for the expected value. Nine is the smallest number of tasks that yields a project standard deviation different from the task standard deviation.

If you write your introduction as you write your model, you will have an extra check on your thinking and you will be able to start your editing early. As you continue your work, you should pause and edit. Rewrite your words when they need it—don't put off the rewriting until the last minute.

Never release a spreadsheet for use until you have read the whole thing on paper. Paper is quiet. Paper is large. Paper allows your eye to range over the entirety of the model. Paper gives your common sense a chance to engage the model's results in a dialogue.

When you feel you have completed your model, allow someone else to test it and proofread it. Listen to his or her responses and revise your work accordingly. Your final model will be better for it.

13. Keep it visible.

A finished model must be written for the reader of the printed version. The decision to use the model is often based on the printed version, so it is critically important that the model make all the facts available to the reader. The model must keep the information visible.

Spreadsheets allow a number of things to be hidden. Formulas and formats lurk behind numbers. Constants can hide in formulas. Named ranges can lie waiting in the framework and never be explained. Graphs can hang on models and not be revealed to the reader. For the on-line user of a simple spreadsheet, these hidden concerns may be only an annoyance. But for the off-line reader of a completed model, all these concerns matter a great deal.

As you work on your model, ask yourself "How will the reader (not the user) know this?" Answer the question by making the idea visible. Tricky formulas can be explained. Unusual formats can be described. Some named ranges can be included in the table of contents, others can be collected in an alphabetical index. Graphs can be listed at the beginning of the graphing section.

If you seriously try to create a model whose printed version you can read and understand, you will succeed in keeping your ideas visible. A great many models fail because their authors wrote for the user of the model and not for the reader of the model. The user is important, and you are not forgetting him or her when you write for the reader. In fact, quite the contrary: if you write for the reader, you will help the user as well . The user is also a reader, and any time saved by reading the facts rather than uncovering them in the model will speed the model's productive use.

14. Space so the spreadsheet may be easily read.

Smooth the path for the reader's eye. Make it easy for him or her to peruse your model. Space paragraphs. Wherever possible, use space between rows or columns rather than lines. Use initial capital letters followed by lower-case letters in most titles. When you use lines or double lines to separate items, make them a symbol of something important: the models in this book use a single line to border the bottom of an area, and a double line to border the bottom of a submodel.

In general, keep models to the left side of the page, where the reader expects to begin a new area or a new paragraph. Most of the models in this book are arranged vertically so that the next section of a model appears below the current one. This vertical arrangement makes it easier to conclude a paragraph with a blank line, an area with a dashed line.

A note of caution about spacing. Spacing within the body of a block of numbers in the model area should be included late in the model's development, if at all. When you revise a model and try to copy a formula down an interrupted column, or to connect a graphing area to a model with an interrupted row, you will notice the inconvenience of the inserted spaces. If you do insert spaces into the body of a block of numbers—say at every tenth line to make the numbers easier to read—do it just before you put the model to bed. If you wake the model up for a different day's work, remove the blank lines to reestablish contiguous blocks of numbers before you begin inserting new rows, deleting old columns, and copying formulas across and down.

YOUR OWN READER

More than all but the most frequent user, you will be the reader of your own spreadsheets. If you begin with a careful design and test your results, if you keep your ideas visible and are kind to your reader's eye, you will greatly speed your own work. This speed is the consequence of being kind to yourself, to your own mind's eye.

4

OTHER FUNCTIONS, OTHER FORMS

*Three wise men of Gotham
Went to sea in a bowl;
If the bowl had been stronger
My song had been longer.*

The basic three-part spreadsheet—Introduction, Initial Data Area, and Model Area—can only go so far. As you work with spreadsheets a variety of quite complex tasks will require different actions and additional areas. You will need other forms for other functions.

15. Give a new function a new area.

The esthetic of the larger spreadsheet is that distinct activities deserve distinct areas. This does not always happen; some people do not know how to keep a large number of regions under control with a table of contents and a map. Others think this is too much extra work to put into a "simple" spreadsheet. Most still do not understand how important it is to make a model easy to modify later on.

As soon as someone suggests that a model should be easy to modify, giving a new function a new area becomes a reasonable idea. If modification means a change in some function, then the part to change is easy to locate: it is the area where the current function takes place. When you want to alter a report, you go to the report area. When you want to change a graph, you modify the graph and perhaps the graphing area in the spreadsheet. When you want to alter a macro, you go to the macro area. Giving a new function a new area is a simple way to let form follow function.

When this idea was applied to computer programs in the early 1970s, experience showed that the programs could be modified in half the time. Because modifying programs accounted for 80% of the cost of programming, cutting this cost in half represented an overall saving of 40% of the effort in working with a computer program!

The following map from a project management spreadsheet shows how powerful this idea can be in practice.

Strong

MAP
Introduction   Input area
Initial data
Report area
 Report on budgeted project by task
 Report on budgeted project by week
 Report on budgeted project by worker
 Report on actual project to date by task
 Report on actual project to date by week
 Report on actual project to date by worker
 Report of budget versus actual, by week, worker, and task.
Graphing Area
 Project budgeted versus actual
 Bar chart of workers actual
Macro Area
 Queries on the database
 Choosing a report to print
Project database

We can see from the map alone where new functions grow in new areas. These areas address two kinds of functions. First, the generic behavior of the spreadsheet leads to areas such as database, graphics, and macros. Second, within these areas the requirements of business require special places for a particular report or a special graph. The map shows that the project database is at the bottom of the spreadsheet. The information in the database is collected in a series of reports. The graphing area collects those items that need to be graphed. The macro area contains those macros necessary to smooth the work of the program.

If someone needs a different report on workers and their actual accomplishments, you know right where to go to begin your work: the "Report on actual project to date by worker." (If the report area fully documents its ties to other areas, you will also know if you must explore the graph area and the macro area for related details.)

If the need arises to revise one of the charts or graphs that this spreadsheet produces, you know to look in the graphing area. If a new week's data arrives, you know where to go to enter it in the database.

Because the spreadsheet grew new business functions (the reports) in new areas, when the business need changes the spreadsheet will change in the appropriate area.

A final note on major and minor functions. The dominating assumption in the foregoing discussion is that the whole spreadsheet was devoted to one major business function. If, in the course of combining activities in one physical spreadsheet, you find two or more distinct business functions, subordinate spreadsheet function to business function.

Weak	Strong
Introduction	Introduction
Initial data	Submodel for business function 1
Data for business function 1	Initial data
Data for business function 2	Model area
Model area	Report A
Model of business function 1	Graphing area
Model of business function 2	Chart A
Report area	Chart B
Report A on business function 1	Macro A
Report B on business function 2	
Report C on business function 2	Submodel for business function 2
Graphing area	Initial data
Chart A on business function 1	Model area
Chart B on business function 1	Report area
Chart C on business function 2	Report B
Chart D on business function 2	Report C
Macro area	Graphing Area
Macro A on business function 1	Chart C
Macro B on business function 2	Chart D
	Macro B

Business function is more important than spreadsheet function because changes in business function drive changes in your spreadsheets. (Only rarely will changes in spreadsheets drive changes in business.) To modify a spreadsheet quickly, it should be organized to respond to changes in business function.

16. Report to your reader.

The purpose of a report is to communicate as clearly and concisely as possible with a particular reader. Think about your reader as you fashion the report. If he or she is interested in your report, you may put the important points last; if not, put them first. If a reader likes to know when the report was made, include the date and time. If the reader already is familiar with a certain style or layout, present the information in that style. Remember that if the reader does not read the report, he or she won't receive the information you wish to convey. Your report should arrest the eye, engage the attention, and win the conviction of your reader.

If you allow yourself a region for each report, you will give yourself the elbow room you need to fashion crisp, appropriate, compelling reports. If you try to format one basic model to please all your readers, you may end up pleasing none.

What you say and how you say it will vary with whom you wish to say it to. Nevertheless, here is a short list to help you to remember the essentials:

1. Lay out your report in a familiar style: conform to department practices.
2. Lay it out in an appealing style.
3. Use typographic variation for emphasis.
4. Include the name of the company and the work group within the company where appropriate.
5. Give a full, accurate title.
6. Include the date and, usually, the time.
7. Introduce the report in plain English.
8. Reference related graphs, macros and models when appropriate.
9. Include information on how to contact the author when appropriate.
10. Group numbers that must be compared.
11. Abbreviate numbers to their useful level of significance.
12. Go from row causes to column effects.
13. Work from left to right—the way the reader reads.
14. Have the reader proofread the report for content and format before it becomes official.

Strong

12-Jun-60	OUR DEPARTMENT'S QUARTERLY PERFORMANCE FOR MONTH OF MAY (Month 2 of Quarter 2)				
	Quarter to date			Until end of quarter	
	Plan	Actual	Rate	Plan	To go
Sales	58	54.0	93%	79.0	25.0
Costs	40.6	39.5	97%	57.8	18.3
Profits	17.4	14.5	83%	21.2	6.7

We are close to being on target.   Let's keep up the good work!
The third month will be a big one. We can make our sales target if we
continue at the level of the last two months. Let's go for it!

Here's a straightforward report. It contains the date it was printed. It is in the format that this department expects to see. It contains a few words of interpretation and encouragement. The numbers that are being compared are close together and clearly labeled. The same basic report might appear in different wrapping in different departments. Here are two alternatives:

Strong

NURSERY KINGDOM   *** CONFIDENTIAL INFORMATION ***

Spreadsheet name: DEPT-BUDG
    Last revised : 3 June 1560
Last revised by: M. Contrary
            Date: 12 June 1560
        Division: Outdoor
            Dept: Garden

	GARDEN DEPARTMENT'S QUARTERLY PERFORMANCE FOR MONTH OF MAY (Month 2 of Quarter 2)				
	Quarter to date			Until end of quarter	
	Plan	Actual	Rate	Plan	To go
Sales	58	54.0	93%	79.0	25.0
Costs	40.6	39.5	97%	57.8	18.3
Profits	17.4	14.5	83%	21.2	6.7

The first of these alternatives has a definite form that identifies the company, division, department, who is currently responsible for the results and when the relevant work was performed.

Strong

Outdoor division, Garden Department   **NURSERY KINGDOM**

Printed on: 12 June 1560	DEPT-BUDG	:Source spreadsheet
	M. Contrary	:Last modified by
	OG5-375566.1	:Document number
	Unclassified	:Classification

GARDEN DEPARTMENT'S QUARTERLY PERFORMANCE
FOR MONTH OF MAY (Month 2 of Quarter 2)

| | Quarter to date | | | Until end of quarter | | |
	Plan	Actual	Rate	Plan	To go	Rate
Sales	58	54.0	93%	79.0	25.0	68%
Costs	40.6	39.5	97%	57.8	18.3	68%
Profits	17.4	14.5	83%	21.2	6.7	68%

The second alternative is another form that might be familiar to the corporate reader. Note that this version includes a document number, and an explicit location for the classification of the document.

When you present two-dimensional tables, remember that a person reads *from row causes to column results*. Consider the following table and two possible reports.

Strong

Model
Observed cell counts

	Elves	Fairies	Goblins	Trolls	Total
Unicorns	9	7	2	0	18
Griffins	3	6	9	2	20
Dragons	1	2	5	8	16
Total	13	15	16	10	54

The model itself betrays a prejudice that mythical beasts pick their mythical masters. When the report from this model is prepared it could look like this.

Strong

18-Nov-90

PETS CHOOSE THEIR MASTERS

	Elves	Fairies	Goblins	Trolls	Total
Unicorns	50%	39%	11%	0%	100%
Griffins	15%	30%	45%	10%	100%
Dragons	6%	12%	31%	50%	100%

Notice that the title of the report—"Pets choose their masters"—describes how the row cause affects the column results. The percentages are displayed across the page so that the reader can compare the actors, the pets.

The initial information allows an alternative interpretation: masters could choose their pets. You could assert this by arranging the same data in a different way.

Strong

18-Nov-90

MASTERS CHOOSE THEIR PETS

	Unicorns	Griffins	Dragons	Total
Elves	69%	23%	8%	100%
Fairies	47%	40%	13%	100%
Goblins	12%	56%	31%	100%
Trolls	0%	20%	80%	100%

Here the reverse assertion is made in the title and supported by the row-cause, column-effect arrangement of the report. Again, the percentages across make it easy to compare the actors. If you wanted to compare effects, you would run percentages down the columns.

Sometimes a report can use a little help. Here is a report on current-year-to-date selling efficiency that make reference to a graph that provides the background of the last twelve months' behavior.

Strong

12-Jun-86	SALES AND SELLING COSTS, MONTH OF MAY					
	January	February	March	April	May	June
Sales	16.00	20.00	21.00	27.00	27.00	0.00
Costs	5.50	5.50	5.50	6.00	6.00	0.00
Costs as % of sales	34%	28%	26%	22%	22%	0%
Smoothed(5 mth)*						
Sales	21.4	22	22.2	25	27	0
Costs as % of sales	26%	25%	25%	24%	22%	0%

*Next-to-last month is smoothed over 3 months, last month is unsmoothed.
Note: This report is supported by the graph "Selling efficiency improves slightly in last 6 months."

Selling efficiency improves slightly in last six months

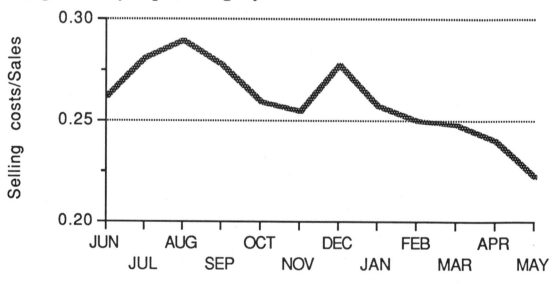

Last 12 months, current month is May

Here the graph backs up the report's information on the first five months of the current year with the trend for the last twelve months. Note that the author of the graph tells the reader in the title what the important point of the graph is: "Selling efficiency improves slightly in last 6 months." This chart could be further improved by reversing the vertical scale so an improvement appears as an upward movement on the chart.

Sometimes a small detail can add a lot to a report. Notice the use of asterisks in the next two examples, the same report in June and again in August.

Strong

10-Jul-35	PERFORMANCE THROUGH MONTH OF JUNE							
	Quarterly performance ***				Half performance ******		Year *	
	Qtr 1	Qtr 2	Qtr 3	Qtr 4	Half 1	Half 2	To date	To end
Planned	44	46	54	72	90	126	90	216
Actual	47	44	0	0	91	0	91	91
Ahead (behind)	3	(2)	—	—	1	—	1	(125)
% of plan	107%	96%	0%	0%	101%	0%	101%	42%

10-Sep-35	PERFORMANCE THROUGH MONTH OF AUGUST							
	Quarterly performance **				Half performance **		Year *	
	Qtr 1	Qtr 2	Qtr 3	Qtr 4	Half 1	Half 2	To date	To end
Planned	44	46	54	72	90	126	129	216
Actual	47	44	41	0	91	41	132	132
Ahead (behind)	3	(2)	(13)	—	1	(85)	3	(84)
% of plan	107%	96%	76%	0%	101%	33%	102%	61%

The asterisks reinforce visually how much data is being reported: in June, all of the quarter, all of the half, some of the year to date; in August, two-thirds of a quarter, two-sixths of the second half, some of the year to date. The asterisk illustrates what it means to have completed the year through June, and in the second example, through August.

A report can help the reader by not including greater numerical accuracy than is warranted.

26-Nov-40   ESTIMATED PROJECT COMPLETION TIME

       6 Number of activities on the project critical path
   137.5 Project mean completion time (50-50 chance)
    28.0 Project completion time standard deviation

PROJECT COMPLETION TIME TABLE

Time:	54	102	114	123	131	138
Probability:	~0%	10%	20%	30%	40%	50%

Time:	138	144	152	161	173	221
Probability:	50%	60%	70%	80%	90%	~100%

The above report includes one decimal place when showing the project mean and standard deviation, but when it gets to the table of days, the numbers are rounded off to realistic whole days. In a 138-day project, it would be silly to talk about tenths of a day. The extra accuracy in the mean and standard deviation allows the reader, by consulting a table of normal distribution figures, to verify independently that the calculations in the time table are correct. The table itself allows the user to see quickly that the job will be done in 138 days, plus or minus 28 days. If the person doing the estimate is new, then the reader can assume the project will probably run long.

When a report draws on data in more than one submodel, the report area can become a submodel in its own right. The last submodel in the spreadsheet NEWBUD is a report. (See the discussion of submodels later in this chapter for a full explanation of the next example.)

                        20-Jan-10
        Corporate Financial Ratios

Asset turnover	2.07
Profit as a % of sales	9.6%
Return on assets	19.8%
Return on equity	16.2%

The report itself is terse. It will be included in an annual report where the surrounding text will explain the importance of the ratios. Knowing the context of a report affects what goes into it.

17. Graph to illuminate.

A graph should shed light on fundamental ideas. Some graphs brilliantly summarize enormous amounts of data. Some pictorially represent a few simple numbers for an important reader who must be made aware of the numbers' importance. Most are concerned with the patterns of things, sales over time, markets over regions, variables causing other variables to do something, parts of the whole, the general line in the cloud of particular points. A picture, however, is not always worth a thousand words. In fact, some pictures require a thousand words before they make sense. If you would have your pictures speak for you, be clear about what you want them to say.

Your job is to be sure you are presenting the pattern in a way that elicits the proper response from your reader. An effective graph achieves the appropriate reaction from the reader. A graph is a special kind of report and a short checklist can help you to remember the essentials:

1. Lay it out in a familiar style: conform to department practices.
2. Lay it out in an appealing style: seduce the viewer's eye.
3. Put your major conclusion in your title.
4. Have the reader proofread the graph for content and format before it becomes official.

Because computer graphing allows heretofore difficult graphing to be done quickly and easily, you will find you are pioneering with new forms when you do some of your graphs. If you are breaking new ground, be careful to do a good job with your graphs. Well-received graphs have a way of becoming the standard, and you will help everyone if your candidates for standards are the best possible pictures.

The foundation of a good graph is the appropriate data in the proper arrangement. In order to ensure this arrangement, you should establish a graphing area in your spreadsheets and base your charts and graphs on this area. The effort you expend to set up this area will be repaid in the freedom you achieve to draw the right graph.

Strong

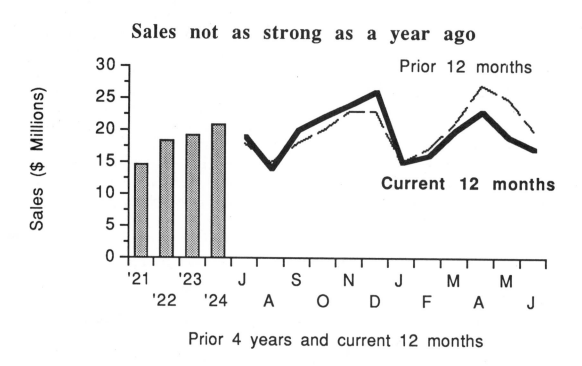

Sales not as strong as a year ago

Prior 12 months

Current 12 months

Sales ($ Millions)

Prior 4 years and current 12 months

Here's a graph that conveys a large amount of information in a small area. It shows what the most recent twelve months of data are: cyclic in nature with highs in December and April. The long-term trend can be inferred from the past years' bars: sales are up over several years (1621–1624). A recent problem is highlighted by the comparison with the prior twelve months' data: recent sales are off. The main point the author wants to make is explicitly stated in the title of the graph: "Sales not as strong as a year ago."

SALES   21 July 1625   S. Simon

Sales figures for Bear Division   ($ Millions)

To add a new month:
1. Add the figure to the raw data for 1625.
2. Erase the left-hand end of the rolling twelve-month table in the graphing section.
3. Shift the graphing variables to the left one month.
4. Add the new month at the right-hand end of the rolling twelve-month table.
5. Be sure the graphs are still well defined.
6. Plot the graphs.

Contents: (each section is a named range)
INTRO   Introduction: Title, description, contents, and map.
INITIAL Initial data and beginning assumptions
GRAPH   Graphing area

Initial data and beginning assumptions

Month	J	F	M	A	M	J	J	A	S	O	N	D
1621	10	14	16	18	20	16	15	13	11	13	14	15
1622	10	15	19	20	21	20	19	15	17	20	22	21
1623	12	17	19	23	22	19	18	15	18	20	23	23
1624	15	17	21	27	25	20	19	14	20	22	24	26
1625	15	16	20	23	19	17						

Graphing area
1. Sales 12 months: last 12, prior 12, and back years' sales figures.

				1st Mth											12th Mth
	21	22	23	24	J	A	S	O	N	D	J	F	M	A	M	J
Curr					19	14	20	22	24	26	15	16	20	23	19	17
	14.6	18.2	19.1	20.8												
Prior					18	15	18	20	23	23	15	17	21	27	25	20

By establishing a graphing section, SALES gives you the freedom to do several things. First, you can make a row of labels for the x-axis that appears just the way you want it to. You could alter the labels to be the full names of the months that begin the year's quarters, January, April, July, and October. Because you are working in the graphing section, you know you are not messing up a printed report when you fiddle with the month names.

Second, you can maintain a rolling twelve-month graph without disturbing the convenient format of the raw data. A rolling twelve-month graph could be a major inconvenience to a person who was maintaining a graph drawn on the raw data. By establishing a graphing area, you allow the data to be manipulated in a convenient way from month to month, so that the spreadsheet can continue being useful after it has been turned over to someone else to use.

Third, you can assemble the information for the average annual bars in exactly the right format for our graphing routine. These average annual bars illustrate how a demanding format for a final graph can be accommodated if you allow yourself the freedom of a separate graphing area. Without the separate graphing area you might not even believe it possible to construct this graph. The separate area allows you to push to their limits the graphing tools at your disposal.

The next example illustrates that the graphing area may be the home of special calculations necessary to produce the right picture.

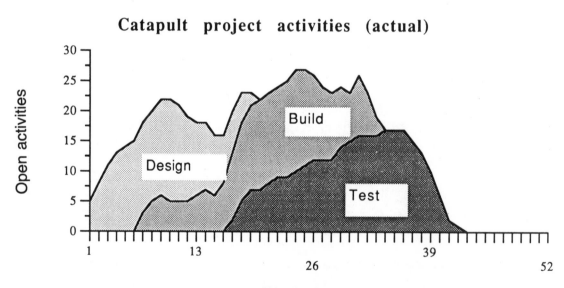

The graph tells a story about building a catapult. Activities were counted as design, build, or test activities. The total number of activities open at any one time was never greater than twenty-seven. When the project began, everyone was designing the catapult. In the sixth week some building activity started. By the seventeenth week building was going full swing, a little late design was being finished up, and a little early testing of some components was beginning. Testing and building went on together, testing becoming the dominant activity by the thirty-third week. The last weeks were exclusively given over to completing the testing, which occurred during the forty-third week.

The graph depends on the number of open activities. This number depends in turn upon the difference between the cumulative number of activities opened and closed. The graphing area looks like this:

Strong

Graphing area

Graphs include:
1. "Open activity"
2. "Total activity"

Cumulative counts

Week number	1	2	3	4	5	6	7	8	9	10	11	12	13	14	15	16	17	18	19	20	21
Design activities																					
Assigned	5	11	18	25	32	40	47	53	59	64	68	72	75	78	81	83	85	86	86	86	86
Completed	0	3	7	12	18	25	32	38	43	47	52	58	63	67	71	75	78	81	84	86	86
Build activities																					
Assigned	0	0	0	0	0	0	3	7	12	16	20	25	31	38	43	49	56	63	70	78	85
Completed	0	0	0	0	0	0	0	2	6	11	15	20	25	31	37	41	45	50	56	63	70
Test activities																					
Assigned	0	0	0	0	0	0	0	0	0	0	0	0	0	0	0	0	2	5	8	11	15
Completed	0	0	0	0	0	0	0	0	0	0	0	0	0	0	0	0	0	0	1	4	7
Total activities																					
Assigned	5	11	18	25	32	40	50	60	71	80	88	97	106	116	124	132	143	154	164	175	186
Completed	0	3	7	12	18	25	32	40	49	58	67	78	88	98	108	116	123	131	141	153	163
Open activities																					
Design	5	8	11	13	14	15	15	15	16	17	16	14	12	11	10	8	7	5	2	0	0
Build	0	0	0	0	0	0	3	5	6	5	5	5	6	7	6	8	11	13	14	15	15
Test	0	0	0	0	0	0	0	0	0	0	0	0	0	0	0	0	2	5	7	7	8
Total (check)	5	8	11	13	14	15	18	20	22	22	21	19	18	18	16	16	20	23	23	22	23
Week axis label	1												13								

Again you see how the separate graphing area provides the necessary freedom to arrange the information in an appropriate manner for the proper pictures. The graph names are listed at the beginning of the Graphing Area. Notice that some simple formulas lurk behind the figures in the Graphing Area. The cumulative figure is the prior cumulative figure plus the current week's value. Open activities are the difference between cumulative assigned and cumulative completed. At some point, if the number and complexity of the formulas increased, they might be separated into a Model Area where they could be arranged so they would be easier to understand.

The next graph discloses an underlying pattern not obvious in the raw numbers.

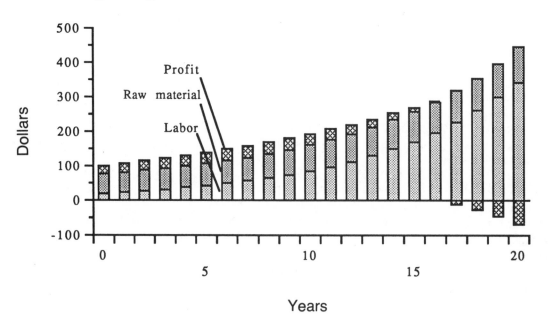

Fast-growing cost becomes the dominant cost

This chart from the model INFLATE shows how the initially small cost, labor, grows to dominate the cost structure of the product. In order to maintain a profit, the price must follow the high-growth cost component more closely as it becomes the dominant cost. In the above example, a 6.8% price growth rate leads to losses beginning in the seventeenth year. The point of the graph is spelled out in its title, "Fast-growing cost becomes the dominant cost." The pattern that is clear in the graph is hidden in the table of numbers:

Graphing Section

YEAR	MATERIAL	LABOR	TOTL COST	PRICE	PROFIT	MARGIN
0	56	21	77	100	23.00	23.0%
	57.68	24.15	81.83	106.83	25.00	23.4%
	59.41	27.77	87.18	114.13	26.95	23.6%
	61.19	31.94	93.13	121.93	28.80	23.6%
	63.03	36.73	99.76	130.26	30.51	23.4%
5	64.92	42.24	107.16	139.17	32.01	23.0%
	66.87	48.57	115.44	148.68	33.23	22.4%
	68.87	55.86	124.73	158.84	34.10	21.5%
	70.94	64.24	135.18	169.69	34.51	20.3%
	73.07	73.88	146.94	181.28	34.34	18.9%
10	75.26	84.96	160.22	193.67	33.46	17.3%
	77.52	97.70	175.22	206.91	31.69	15.3%
	79.84	112.36	192.20	221.04	28.85	13.1%
	82.24	129.21	211.45	236.15	24.70	10.5%
	84.71	148.59	233.29	252.29	18.99	7.5%
15	87.25	170.88	258.12	269.53	11.40	4.2%
	89.86	196.51	286.37	287.94	1.57	0.5%
	92.56	225.99	318.55	307.62	− 10.93	− 3.6%
	95.34	259.88	355.22	328.64	− 26.58	− 8.1%
	98.20	298.87	397.06	351.10	− 45.97	− 13.1%
20	101.14	343.70	444.84	375.09	− 69.75	− 18.6%

A reader looking at this table of numbers would stare at it for several days before seeing the pattern of labor costs that leaps to the eye in the graph. The graph illuminates the important idea.

Sometimes a very simple chart can help explain a position. The following chart tells a department how things are going two months through the quarter. This information is very interesting to people whose bonuses ride on making the goals.

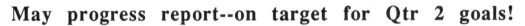

May progress report--on target for Qtr 2 goals!

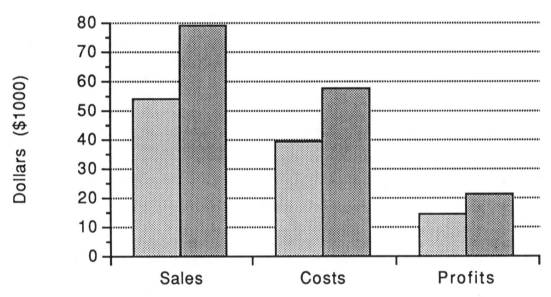

While this graph contains very little information and might justifiably be considered a poor graph for most purposes, it is an excellent chart to post on the wall to tell everyone what has been done, and what remains to be done, to hit the quarterly goals. During the final month, someone could pencil in progress on the chart.

The next example shows how a graph can present a great deal in a small space.

This chart shows the raw data of the last twelve months, the seasonally adjusted data of the same period, the best-fit line to the seasonally adjusted data, the projected value for the next month, and the predicted raw value. It is a good graph because it condenses lots of information into a compact, meaningful whole.

September sales predicted from seasonally adjusted data

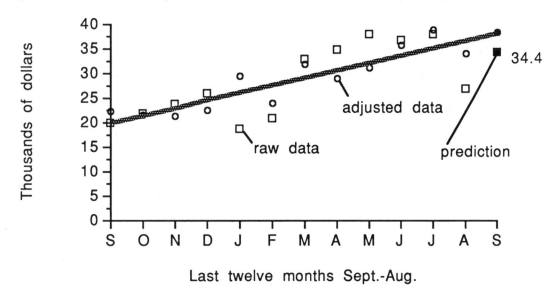

The portion of the graphing area on which the graph was based looks like this:

Strong

Graphing section:
1. "Next month's sales"
2. "Seasonal factors"
Next month's sales

x-label	x(i)	y(i)	s(i)	Line	s(13)	y(13)
S	1	20	22.3	20.1		
O	2	22	21.5	21.6		
N	3	24	21.2	23.1		
D	4	26	22.5	24.6		
J	5	19	29.4	26.2		
F	6	21	24.1	27.7		
M	7	33	31.9	29.2		
A	8	35	29.0	30.7		
M	9	38	31.2	32.3		
J	10	37	35.7	33.8		
J	11	38	38.7	35.3		
A	12	27	34.1	36.8		
S	13			38.4	38.4	34.4

Again you see a list of the graphs by name and a column of labels set up to help the graph. Notice also that the area uses a whole column to get s(13) and y(13) on the graph exactly the way it wants.

Sometimes a large amount of data can be reduced to a series of graphs that tell a story. The next three graphs summarize a model with over 330 equations. The model lets three firms compete for a growing market for ten years. Firm A wants to capture a large share of the market, Firm B wants to preserve its initial one-third of the market, and Firm C is willing to give up its share in exchange for a few years of high prices. All three firms begin at the same place.

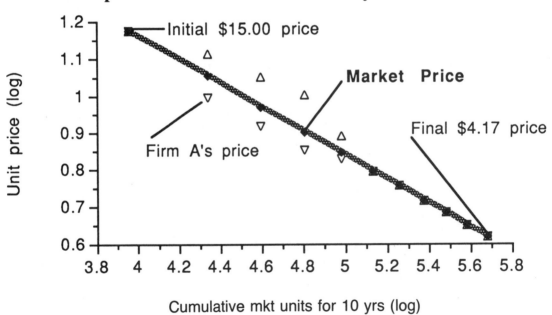

Firm A prices below the market for four years . . .

Unit price (log)

1.2 — Initial $15.00 price

Market Price

Firm A's price

Final $4.17 price

Cumulative mkt units for 10 yrs (log)

to gain a dominant market share . . .

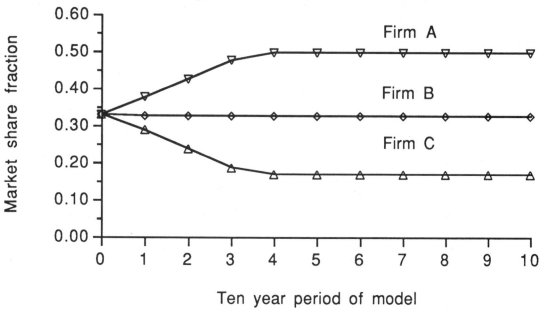

and reap huge long-term rewards.

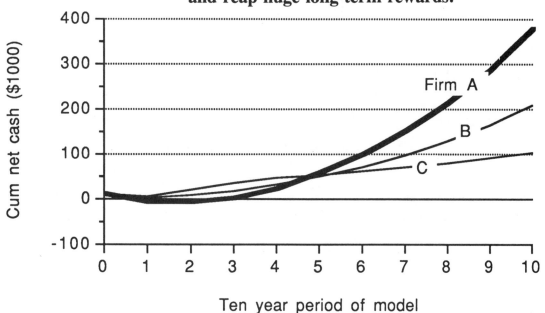

Notice that the first plot uses the logarithms of some data in order to show the price decline as a straight line function of the cumulative market volume. The place where the logarithms are computed is in the graphing area. If data that you graph can be more clearly revealed if you transform it, the graphing area will give you a place to do your transformations.

The final graph in this section is a summary of information contained in a report shown earlier. The graph of project completion time shows much more about when the project will end.

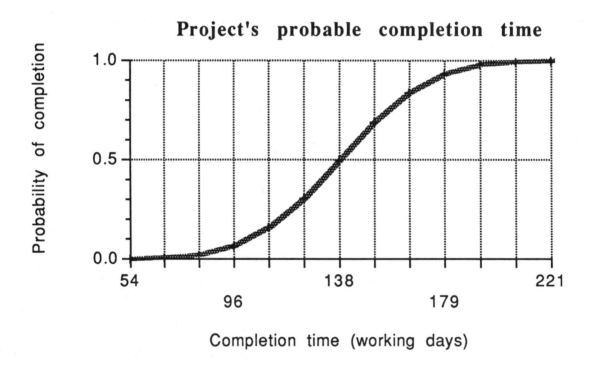

Project's probable completion time

You can see at a glance that if you say you will be done in 179 days, you have more than a 90% chance of being right.

18. Import with care.

When you move data between spreadsheets you are sometimes faced with the dilemma of importing a block of unknown size. A good way to import such a block is to land it on your spreadsheet to the right of your working model. Work imported to this location can be longer and wider than you anticipated without damaging your preexisting work. After you have landed the data safely, you may move it to its final location in your spreadsheet.

Even if your spreadsheet regularly receives a fixed block of information, set it down in your import area before moving it to its final location. This cautious practice will protect you against an unannounced change in size and give you a chance to catch someone else's oversight before it affects your work.

Because the import area is a temporary staging area for information destined to be moved elsewhere on your spreadsheet, it usually consists of two cells.

Strong

Import area
XXXXXXXXX

The XX cell is where you anchor the upper left corner of the block. After you have moved the new information to its final location, erase any leftovers and reenter the XXs before you knock off work for the day. Leave the area as clean as you found it.

You may export a block from anywhere on your spreadsheet. Do, however, take the time to be sure you know the dimensions of what you are exporting.

19. Verify critical work.

When you build large models, you will want to prove to yourself that everything is functioning properly. To be sure of your spreadsheet, you must verify critical work. A good way to guard against error is to build the model defensively by incorporating checks wherever possible.

A second reason to verify your essential work is that you will want to be sure that any change you make in your program—changing a formula in the fifth column, erasing the fourth row, adding a new constant to the initial data—does not alter the important work of the model.

Verifying critical work springs from an attitude that has its roots in fourteenth-century Italian traders who invented double entry bookkeeping to be sure their accounts were in order. A present-day accountant continues to ask whether the figures double check. Did you add the correct number of items? Was the sum correct? Did the row totals agree with the column totals? Was any number out of bounds by being either too large or too small?

In a spreadsheet model you can ask these questions with defensive formulas that have the following form:

If(everything is okay, print the answer, otherwise print "error")

This expression can take many forms:

Weak	Strong
Positive number +A67	Positive number @IF(A67$\geq$0,A67,@ERR)
Monthly salary +B20	Monthly salary @IF((B20$\geq$1000)#AND#(B20$\leq$30000),B20, @ERR)
Grand total of A1..S99 @SUM(A1..S99)	Grand Total of A1..S99 @IF(@SUM(T1..T99)=@SUM(A100..S100), @SUM(A1..S99),@ERR)
Sum of 100 Entries where the value 100 is in cell A5 @SUM(A56..A155)	Sum of 100 Entries where the value 100 is in cell A5 @IF(@COUNT(A56..A155)=A5, @SUM(A56..A155),@ERR)

You may think of these defensive formulas as warning lights. The positive number warning turns to error when the number goes negative. The monthly salary warning goes off when someone makes less than $12,000 a year or more than $360,000 a year. The grand total warning is triggered if the column of row totals does not cross check with the row of column totals. The sum of a fixed number (100) of entries is wrong if there are not exactly the right number of entries. (The fixed number is an initial datum stored in A5.)

Be careful with checks of equality and cross-checked sums in particular. Sometimes two sums will not be equal because of computer round-off error. The two totals will differ by a tiny amount that you will only see if you subtract the one quantity from the other. The difference may be as small as .00000000001. The safe way to ask if two numbers are equal is to ask if they differ by an insignificant amount. Because you won't know which is the bigger number, you should ask about the absolute value of the difference. If the absolute value of the difference is less than a tiny number then the numbers are "equal." The way to say that in a spreadsheet formula is:

If (absolute value(sum − check sum) < .000001,
    print sum, print "error")

Strong

Grand Total of A1..S99
@IF(@ABS(@SUM(T1..T99) − @SUM(A100..S100)) < .000001, @SUM(A1..S99),@ERR)

The strong formula works in all cases where the difference is less than one part in a million. You may need to experiment to determine what small number is appropriate to your spreadsheet. If you are at all unsure what to use, ask someone who knows about computer round-off errors to help you.

You may be interested in only the relative error between two numbers. The formula for making sure the error is less that a tenth of a percent is:

If (absolute value(1 − (sum/check sum)) < .001,
    print sum, print "error")

In a large model, after you have established your warning lights, you may find it convenient to collect them into a "control panel" that will let you know quickly whether or not any of your warning lights have been set off. You may do this by establishing a verify area.

Strong

Verify area

34,470,527   The model verification sum

If an error appears here, check below and then the appropriate area of the model. (Be sure you have recalculated the whole model.)

347,000	The raw data cross check
666,352	The model cross check
375	The number of items in the report
33,456,777	The sum of all the checked values in the database
23	The number of graphed periods

This verify area collects several warning lights in one place. If a cross check fails, an "error" appears in the individual listing and in the model verification sum. The verification sum is a nonsense number that uses the sum function as a quick way to detect if any item in the sum has gone bad.

Strong

Verify area

ERR   The model verification sum

If an error appears here, check below and then the appropriate area of the model. (Be sure you have recalculated the whole model.)

347,000	The raw data cross check
666,352	The model cross check
ERR	The number of items in the report
33,456,777	The sum of all the checked values in the database
23	The number of graphed periods

In the above example the verify sum model check is flashing "error." The individual item is from the report area. When you go to the report area, you will see the "error" warning there and you may correct the problem. Notice that the directions for the verify area include a reminder to recalculate the model before assuming that the warning lights are valid.

If you know of other corrective actions for your particular model, include them in the verify area.

20. Control all macros.

A macro can be a source of convenient help or a burden of confusing clutter. It is intended to help save typing time by allowing you to abbreviate several key-strokes to a single keystroke. A macro also allows the author of a model to simplify things for the eventual user. The extent to which you engage in writing macros is directly related to who will be using the spreadsheet and how you want them to use it. On the one hand, a macro can make possible an application that might otherwise be too time-consuming. On the other hand, a macro must be expressed in a sloppy programming language that is fraught with perils. A macro will be useful only if you keep it under strict control.

The first level of control you should exhibit over macros is when to write one. Write as few macros as possible. If you have a choice between making the spread-sheet clearer for the reader by documenting a feature or automating it with a macro, document it. Macros are hard to read; documentation is easy. The likeli-hood that the model will be reusable is much higher if you are clearly communi-cating with your reader.

The second level of control is to collect the macros you write in an area devoted to macros. Frequently this area will be at the bottom of the spreadsheet. Being at the bottom gets them out of harm's way. Here you may add additional length and not disturb the rest of the spreadsheet. If they appear in their own area, macros are more likely to be surrounded by appropriate comment.

The third level of control is the documentation you bring to the macro. Macros are a frightfully terse form of expression. This imbues them with great power, but also with great mystery. To understand your own work, let alone to explain what you did to a second reader, requires careful attention to the details of your comment.

Weak	Strong	
Macro area	Macro area	
/fs~r	\R ~	Replace a file macro
	/fs~r	

The documentation here consists of two comments on either side of the macro's first cell, which contains a tilde (~). The \R comment indicates that the cell to its right has a range name of \R. Without the \R comment on the left, the reader has no idea that the cell containing the tilde is the beginning of a macro called \R. (Macros begin in cells with two-character range names that are a backslash (\) followed by a letter of the alphabet. The comment to the right explains the macro—"Replace a file macro." If you do not understand macros, consult a guide to 1-2-3™, Version 1A, to learn about the conventions employed here.) A reasonable style for range names is to always label the cell to the left of the one that is range named. Because of the left-hand labels, strong macros go down column B with comments going down column A. When an extended remark is necessary, it can be placed on the same line, in a cell to the right of the macro command.

Weak	Strong	
Macro area	Macro area	
/dt1f13..i16~c3~	\D ~	Data table definition
	/dt1DATATABLE1~INPUTCELL1~	

This example shows how a macro can save the settings for producing a table of summary data by saving the set of commands necessary to query the database. (See the 1-2-3™, Version 1A, explanation of data tables.) With one keystroke you can invoke the first data table.

This example also shows how a macro can create a feature that the spreadsheet tool lacks. The spreadsheet allows you to save different combinations of settings for graphs, but does not allow you to save different settings for printing reports, or for producing tables of summary data from databases. With this macro a single keystroke will invoke the first of what could be several different data tables.

The strong examples also illustrate the fourth, fifth, and sixth levels of control. They keep each line of macros short to aid both comprehension and editing. There is only one command on the line. They distinguish commands (lower case) from areas acted upon (upper case). They also use range names for all areas in the spreadsheet. The data table f13..i16 has been named DATABLE1, and c3 has become INPUTCELL1. Range names preserve your freedom to move areas on your spreadsheet because range names move with the areas while cell names do not.

A seventh level of control is to keep the macro area under lock and key. The consequences of an inadvertent alteration of a single cell in this region ca be calamitous. *Always keep the Macro Area protected.*

The weak and strong versions of the next example show the cumulative effect of the above rules. Both versions do exactly the same thing, but only the strong version could be used by a second user, and only the strong version could be conveniently modified for extended reuse.

Weak

Macro area
Decision

/xia27>10~True~
False~

Repetition

/dfb33~1~~~
/xib33>12~/xgb123~
This line flashes with each repetition.~
/re~
/dfb33~b33+1~~~
/xgb118~
~

Strong

Macro area

\A The decision (IF...THEN...ELSE) macro
\B The repetition (DO...WHILE) macro

Variables and constants
COUNT   13
HURDLE   10
LIMIT   12
VARIABLE   5

This macro asks the question "Is the variable larger than the hurdle?"

\A	~	This is a decision structure.
IF	/xiVARIABLE>HURDLE~/xgIFTRUE~	
	/xgIFFALSE~	
IFTRUE	~	
	True~	
	/xgIFEND~	
IFFALSE	~	
	False~	
IFEND	~	

This macro flashes a line until the count exceeds the limit.

\B	~	This is a repetition structure.
LOOPTOP	/dfCOUNT~1~~~	
LOOPBEGIN	/xiCOUNT>LIMIT~/xgLOOPEND~	
	This line flashes with each repetition.~	
	/re~	
	/dfCOUNT~COUNT+1~~~	
	/xgLOOPBEGIN~	
LOOPEND	~	

Notice that the Macro Area, like the Graph Area, contains a table of contents. If you add a new macro to your model every day, a table of contents at the beginning of the macro area helps you find the correct macro.

A fundamental result of computer science is that you can write every computer program with three logical forms: sequence, decision, and repetition. Every macro procedes down the spreadsheet until it encounters a blank line which forces it to stop (sequence). The above example, by illustrating the programming structures IF...THEN...ELSE (decision) and DO...WHILE (repetition), demonstrates that you can write regular computer programs with macro instructions.

If you must write a lot of macros, extend your control by learning as much as you can about computer programming. You should understand the fundamentals of what computer programmers call structured programming and be able to apply it to writing your macros. If you find yourself writing many large macros, see a professional programmer for help.

The strong example illustrates another feature of good programming: each logical form has a single beginning cell and a single ending cell. This enables these forms to appear in a sequence, do their work, and return to the sequence when they are done. The sequence could be inside a repetition or inside a branch of a decision. These forms can be embedded inside one another to create larger forms. Decisions can occur inside loops, loops can occur inside branches of a decision. If you were to make repeated use of an IF structure, the first set of range names could be IF1, IFTRUE1, and so on. The second structure could begin IF2, and so on.

Be sure to note in the strong example that the cell containing the value 5 of VARIABLE and the cell containing the value 13 of COUNT must be unprotected so they may be changed without disabling the protection scheme that covers the rest of the Macro Area.

The next macro allows the user to choose one of three graphs from a menu. The menu explanation tells whether the selections are line, bar, or pie graphs. (See 1-2-3™, Version 1A, explanation of the /xm command.)

Weak

/xmmenu~			
Tulip	Daffodil	Rose	Quit
line of tulip	bar of daffodil	pie of rose	quit
/gnutulip~q~	/gnudaffodil~q~	/gnurose~q~	/xq~
/xmmenu~	/xmmenu~	/xmmenu~	

Strong

This macro allows the user to choose one of three graphs from a menu.

\M	~		
	/xmMENU~		

MENU	Tulip	Daffodil	Rose	Quit
	line of tulip	bar of daffodil	pie of rose	quit
	/gnuTULIP~q~	/gnuDAFFODIL~q~	/gnuROSE~q~	/xgENDMENU~
	/xmMENU~	/xmMENU~	/xmMENU~	

ENDMENU	~

In the weak version, when you quit the menu, the macro stops; but in the strong version the menu goes to its ending cell (named ENDMENU). Because the strong menu has a single beginning cell (named MENU) and a single ending cell (named ENDMENU), it can be entered from a larger macro and return to that macro after it ends. You can easily use the form to construct a pyramid of menus and submenus. Because menus give you a way to write documentation that is familiar to the user, an eighth level of control over macros is to embed the macros in a macro menu. The first choice in the above example might change from "Tulip" to "Graphing Macros" and the actual example would be the first submenu. The second major choice might be "Database Macros," the third, "Printing Macros," and so on. The menus might be organized like this:

```
Macro menu organization
    Graphing menu
        Line graph of Tulip
        Bar chart of Daffodil
        Pie chart of Rose
    Database reports
        Workers by project
        Workers by week
        Projects by week
    Printed reports
        8 1/2 x 11 reports
          Report on workers
          Report on roses
        14 x 11 reports
          Report on projects and weeks
          Report on flowers
```

Should you find yourself deeply involved in writing macros, seriously consider hiring a professional to set up this part of your spreadsheet. Carefully distinguish between those macros you need and those you wish you needed. Always, always, control your macros.

21. Focus the model's activity.

Sometimes a model is written so that a user can systematically vary one of the initial variables and observe the effects on a critical result that is at the far end of the spreadsheet. To look at both numbers easily, the spreadsheet may be split into two windows. If, however, several widely dispersed results must be examined, the window solution becomes inconvenient. The way to resolve this problem is to grow a new area called the *active area* and to treat this area like an animated report that focuses the model's activity.

The active area consists of an attractively formatted copy of the initial data to be varied, along with the appropriate final results. Before beginning the day's activity, the user can reverse the pointing so that the initial data points to the active area. The user may then go to the active area, vary the initial variables to his or her heart's content, print out appropriate findings (the active area has been set up like a report area so the results are printable), and think about those findings. When the user is done, he or she reestablishes the original pointing from the active area to the initial data (or throws away the active version of the spreadsheet) and quits for the day.

Strong

Active area

MANPOWER COVERAGE OF SCHEDULED WORK FOR NEXT FOUR QUARTERS

3 July 1586

| 23 | Manpower available at end of current quarter |
| 2 | Current quarter number |

Scheduled work covered by current manpower

Quarter	Work covered (%)
3	87
4	65
5	110
6	120

Here the user changes the figures for the number of people available and the quarter to see what percentage of the upcoming scheduled work will be covered.

The user might decide to get more people and want to see what effect it has on the project:

Strong

Active area

MANPOWER COVERAGE OF SCHEDULED WORK FOR NEXT FOUR QUARTERS

3 July 1586

25	Manpower available at end of current quarter
2	Current quarter number

Scheduled work covered by current manpower

Quarter	Work covered (%)
3	92
4	75
5	130
6	150

Strong

Active area

MANPOWER COVERAGE OF SCHEDULED WORK FOR NEXT FOUR QUARTERS

3 July 1586

30	Manpower available at end of current quarter
2	Current quarter number

Scheduled work covered by current manpower

Quarter	Work covered (%)
3	102
4	90
5	160
6	175

From these trials the user chooses the last as a reasonable alternative. Note that this active area probably depends on a large, elaborately scheduled model that integrates all the projects the group is working on.

As a general rule, the model should be saved with the initial data in the initial data area. If, however, a particular spreadsheet only exists to perform an active area chore, then the spreadsheet might be profitably rearranged with the active area at the top:

Strong

Contents
    Introduction
    Active area
    Initial data
    Supporting model
    Occasional report
    Rarely used graphing area

This arrangement provides the user with the convenience of quickly getting to the work area. The active area might also be saved in its active state. (But a note to warn the user should also be included in the initial data area. For example, "WARNING: some of the initial data are controlled from the active area.")

Strong

Active area

GNP Growth, Unemployment, and Inflation as a Function
of Monetary Growth(M1) and Fiscal Control(Natl. Debt).   15 Sept 1986

	Year 1	Year 2	Year 3	Year 4	Year 5
M1 growth	10.0%	15.0%	13.0%	11.0%	8.0%
Natl. Debt ($B)	240	160	90	60	0
GNP growth	4.6%	7.6%	5.1%	3.1%	0.0%
Unemployment	6.7%	4.9%	4.3%	4.8%	6.8%
Inflation	4.6%	5.2%	7.5%	6.1%	4.5%

This is an active area that a policy maker can use to manipulate different assumptions about the monetary (M1) growth rate and the national debt to see the effects on gross national product (GNP), unemployment, and inflation. The supporting spreadsheet may well contain pages of calculations, several different kinds of reports, and many charts and graphs. But what the policy maker needs to see, and occasionally needs to print out, are two key assumptions and three critical results. The active area provides just what is needed.

    The impulse behind the active area is to give a casual user an easy way to manipulate the spreadsheet. If you pursue this impulse very far, you will find yourself using macros to prepare for the user, to guide the user through certain tasks, and to help the user end the session. You should consult a book on writing and using macros for help and guidance. If you combine the macro methods you learn there with well-structured spreadsheets, you will provide the casual user with an industrial-strength spreadsheet that will withstand heavy use.

THE SUBMODEL

Sometimes a large spreadsheet gets out of control. Several areas of a large model can depend on each other in such complex ways that the model becomes hard to understand and difficult to modify. Sometimes the activities associated with one part of a model evolve more rapidly than those associated with the rest. Sometimes one part gets used in several different spreadsheets. Sometimes two or more old spreadsheets combine to make one effective new one. Sometimes a spreadsheet gets used by several individuals, each of whom wants to control a part of it. Any one of these events could require the creation of a sound submodel.

   Consider for a moment what you might do to break up a large, complex model into submodels. Converting such a model is a little like performing a condominium conversion on an apartment house—when you are finished you will have the same basic material, but each piece will have a certain independence from the others.

Before	After
Introduction	Introduction
Initial data	Submodel 1
Data for Part 1	Initial and entering data
Data for Part 2	Model
Data for Part 3	Report A
Model	Submodel 2
Part 1	Initial and entering data
Part 2	Model
Part 3	Submodel 3
Report A using Part 1	Initial and entering data
Report B using Parts 2 & 3	Model
Report C using Part 3	Report C
	Submodel 4
	Entering data
	Report B (using Submodels 2 & 3)

This example leads to the fundamental rule of a spreadsheet submodel:

22. Enter carefully.

Any cell of a spreadsheet can be used in a formula somewhere else. Because any cell can appear in any distant formula at any time, a cell is completely vulnerable to uncontrolled exits. If you cannot control a cell's exits, you must control its entrances. You can do this by being sure that everything enters a submodel through its Initial and Entering Data Area.

Entering data can be controlled in a familiar way. Every basic spreadsheet controls data with its Initial Data Area and a submodel does the same. Entrances can be controlled because they are of immediate interest to the author of the submodel. In order to see what the submodel depends on, you must establish an Initial and Entering Data area. Without this area, you cannot independently test the submodel and prove to yourself that it works. When you build a submodel, you must enter carefully.

The logic of spreadsheets asserts that exiting data is inherently unstable. Figure 1 depicts the outflow from Part 1 of a model. Even if you wished to control these

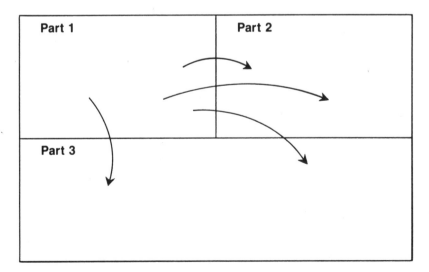

Figure 1. Uncontrolled exits from Part 1 occur when foreign formulas refer to cells in Part 1.

exits by moving them to an exit area at the bottom of Part 1, the next undis-
ciplined author who added a Part 4 could tap into your Part 1 at any point. The
open nature of a spreadsheet renders exiting data impossible to control.

Notice that a spreadsheet gets larger when it is broken into submodels because
all the entering data is labeled in a separate place for the first time. Submodels
also disperse the control from one central location to several locations. In the next
example, a kingdom's spreadsheet will be divided up among three castles.

THREE CASTLE KINGDOM—Step #1
Initial data
    King's flag
    Stone
    Wood
    Red paint
    Yellow paint
    Black paint
Castle Red
    Red walls = stone + red paint
    Red tower = yellow tower copy + stone + red paint
    Red drawbridge = black drawbridge copy + wood + red paint
    Red castle = red walls + red drawbridge + red tower + King's flag
Castle Yellow
    Yellow walls = red wall copy + stone + yellow paint
    Yellow tower = stone + yellow paint
    Yellow drawbridge = black drawbridge copy + wood + yellow paint
    Yellow castle = yellow walls + yellow drawbridge + yellow tower + King's flag
Castle Black
    Black walls = stone + black paint
    Black tower = yellow tower copy + stone + black paint
    Black drawbridge = wood + black paint
    Black castle = black walls + black drawbridge + black tower + King's flag

---

In THREE CASTLE KINGDOM—Step #1, you see some of the model's data flows:
from the initial data to the model (stone, wood), from one location in the initial
data to many parts of the model (King's flag), from one part of the model to
another (red wall copy), from one part of the model to many other parts (black

drawbridge copy), and from many parts of the model to one part (red castle formula).

Step #2 will show the evolution of a large model into three submodels.

THREE CASTLE KINGDOM—Step #2
Castle Red
 Initial data
     King's flag
     Red paint
 Model
     Red walls = stone + red paint
     Red tower = yellow tower copy + stone + red paint
     Red drawbridge = black drawbridge copy + wood + red paint
     Red castle = red walls + red drawbridge + red tower + King's flag
Castle Yellow
 Initial data
     Stone
     Yellow paint
 Model
     Yellow walls = red wall copy + stone + yellow paint
     Yellow tower = stone + yellow paint
     Yellow drawbridge = black drawbridge copy + wood + yellow paint
     Yellow castle = yellow walls + yellow drawbridge + yellow tower + King's flag
Castle Black
 Initial data
     Wood
     Black paint
 Model
     Black walls = stone + black paint
     Black tower = yellow tower copy + stone + black paint
     Black drawbridge = wood + black paint
     Black castle = black walls + black drawbridge + black tower + King's flag

---

Step #2 shows the intermediate partitioning of the model. Notice that here we have a problem with terms in formulas that come from other submodels (the copies of the drawbridge, stone, King's flag). These terms could be nearby or far away. They are not visible locally if you wanted to modify them. If you tried to extract one submodel from the spreadsheet, and remembered to freeze the values in the Initial Data Area, you would still find mysterious errors in the submodel's Model Area. For example an extracted Castle Yellow would look like this:

Weak

Castle Yellow (extracted from THREE CASTLE KINGDOM—Step #2)
 Initial data
    Stone
    Yellow paint
 Model
    Yellow walls = @ERR + stone + yellow paint
    Yellow tower = stone + yellow paint
    Yellow drawbridge = @ERR + @ERR + yellow paint
    Yellow castle = @ERR + @ERR + yellow tower + @ERR

When a submodel is correctly extracted from a large spreadsheet, no error should occur. When Castle Yellow's extracted submodel contains errors in the Model Area, the submodel partitioning has serious problems. The last step resolves these problems.

THREE CASTLE KINGDOM—Step #3
Castle Red
  Initial and entering data
    King's flag
    Red paint
  From Castle Yellow
    Stone
    Yellow tower design
  From Castle Black
    Wood
    Black drawbridge design
  Model
    Red walls = stone + red paint
    Red tower = yellow tower copy + stone + red paint
    Red drawbridge = black drawbridge copy + wood + red paint
    Red castle = red walls + red drawbridge + red tower + King's flag

Castle Yellow
 Initial and entering data
    Stone
    Yellow paint
  From Castle Red
    King's flag
    Red wall design
  From Castle Black
    Wood
    Black drawbridge design
  Model
    Yellow walls = red wall copy + stone + yellow paint
    Yellow tower = stone + yellow paint
    Yellow drawbridge = black drawbridge copy + wood + yellow paint
    Yellow castle = yellow walls + yellow drawbridge + yellow tower + King's flag
Castle Black
 Initial and entering data
    Wood
    Black paint
  From Castle Red
    King's flag
  From Castle Yellow
    Stone
    Yellow tower design
  Model
    Black walls = stone + black paint
    Black tower = yellow tower copy + stone + black paint
    Black drawbridge = wood + black paint
    Black castle = black walls + black drawbridge + black tower + King's flag

In the final Step #3, the Initial and Entering Data Area distinguishes between new data introduced for the first time in the submodel and old data that comes from another submodel. For example, Castle Yellow has its own stone, but it depends on Castle Red for the King's flag and on Castle Black for its wood. The general form of the Initial and Entering Data Area is:

Initial and entering data area
    Raw initial data necessary for this submodel
    Data from another Submodel
    Data from yet another Submodel

While Step #3 continues to have complex data flows, it has established control over them by entering carefully. In every submodel, you can see that stone is quarried near Castle Yellow, wood is lumbered near Castle Black. You know for sure where the design for each part of a castle comes from.

Because all exterior data enters a submodel at the top, references in the body of a submodel stay within the submodel or refer to the Initial and Entering Data Area. The data is visible locally if you wish to modify it locally. If Castle Yellow wanted to modify the "Red wall design," it would:

- move the value from "From Castle Red" to "Initial Data," and
- relabel the value "New wall design."

When data enters the submodel from other submodels, it should continue to be connected to the original source. An initial piece of data should exist in only one submodel's "raw initial data" area and be referred to by every other submodel in its "Entering from . . ." area (for example, the King's flag). If the entering piece of data comes from the body of another submodel, of course you point to the cell where it first appears. (In Castle Yellow's Initial and Entering Data Area, the red wall design points to Castle Red's wall.)

Because every formula in the body of a submodel goes through the Initial and Entering Data area on its way to the original source, the risk of intermediate error is introduced into the spreadsheet. Castle Black could mistakenly modify the design of the Yellow tower and not realize that it was no longer using the design from Castle Yellow. This risk of intermediate error is a high, but reasonable, price to pay for a clear division of the spreadsheet and a firm control of every submodel.

SUBMODELS AND THE REUSE OF TOOLS

Submodels provide you with a larger and more versatile library of tools to use in future models. Because the pieces are set up to become technically independent, you can use them in another context more quickly.

A user can "freeze" the numbers and labels in the Initial and Entering Data Area and cut the submodel out of the large model for independent use. A cut-out submodel can be added to another model, connected where it needs to be, and used with the conviction that it works.

With THREE CASTLE KINGDOM—Step #3 you can extract one submodel and use it on its own. An extracted Castle Yellow might look like this:

Strong

Castle Yellow (extracted from THREE CASTLE KINGDOM—Step #3)
Initial (and entering?)data
    Stone
    Yellow paint
    King's flag
    Red wall design
    Wood
    Black drawbridge design
  From ??
  From ??
Model
    Yellow walls = red wall copy + stone + yellow paint
    Yellow tower = stone + yellow paint
    Yellow drawbridge = black drawbridge copy + wood + yellow paint
    Yellow castle = yellow walls + yellow drawbridge + yellow tower + King's flag

---

In its independent form, all Castle Yellow's Initial and Entering Data becomes Initial Data. Before Castle Yellow is sucessfully inserted in a new spreadsheet, data that come from submodels in the new spreadsheet would be broken out in "From ??" Areas.

A large model broken into submodels differs from a large integrated model because you can reassert full control over each submodel. First, you have intellectual control: each model explains itself to the reader in a way the reader is likely to comprehend and remember. Second, you have physical control: if you want to temporarily exercise just one submodel, you can do so by varying the values in the submodel's Initial and Entering Data area. (This local variation may cut the submodel's ties to other submodels, and the temporary version should be thrown away after use.) Third, you have evolutionary control: by breaking the model into pieces that correspond to business functions (see the earlier discussion under Rule 15 :"Give a new function a new area") you give the future user a better chance to accurately modify the current spreadsheet to a future need. The model is more likely to evolve in concert with the business it is intended to serve.

Below you see a family budget spreadsheet as it might evolve over time. The budget allows each member of the family to earn money. The family has fixed expenses that vary little from month to month. The family also has a few policies: the parents each get an allowance based on their monthly income, the father holds the family's entertainment budget (which is a percentage of the parents' joint earnings), the mother controls the clothing budget for the husband and son, the daughter may spend up to 33% of her earnings on clothes, the son must save 50% of his special earnings, and each child gets a fixed allowance in addition to whatever he or she earns on his or her own.

Weak

FAMILY FINANCE   30 June 1600   B. Bunting
(C) Copyright 1986 by John M. Nevison

Show the family's finances

Contents: (each section is a named range)
INTRO   Introduction: Title, description, contents, and map.
INITIAL   Initial data and beginning assumptions
MODEL   Model

Initial data and beginning assumptions
                5%   Percent of income permitted as parent allowance
                3%   Percent of joint parent income for entertainment
                33%   Percent of Daughter's earnings that may be spent on clothes
                50%   Percent of Son's earnings he must save

| | Springtime | | |
	April	May	June
Father			
Income	1000	900	1050
House	450	450	450
Fuel	200	0	0
Insurance	0	0	250
Mother			
Income	1000	1100	1200
Health ins	300	300	300
Car expenses	200	250	275
Food	200	200	200
Clothing	100	100	100
Son			
Income	0	0	18
Allowance	5	5	5
Daughter			
Income	100	74	130
Allowance	15	15	15

Model

		Springtime		
	April	May	June	Total
Father				
Income	1000	900	1050	2950
House	450	450	450	1350
Fuel	200	0	0	200
Insurance	0	0	250	250
Entertainment at %	60	60	67	187
Allowance at %	50	45	52	147
Total family income	2100	2074	2398	6572
Total family spending	1663	1504	1827	4994
Total family saving	437	570	571	1578
Mother				
Income	1000	1100	1200	3300
Health ins	300	300	300	900
Car expenses	200	250	275	725
Food	200	200	200	600
Clothing	100	100	100	300
Allowance at %	50	55	60	165
Children's spending	53	44	72	169
Son				
Income	0	0	18	18
Allowance	5	5	5	15
Extra spending	0	0	9	9
Daughter				
Income	100	74	130	304
Allowance	15	15	15	45
Clothing allowance	33	24	43	100

This model, while relatively small, has quite a few complex dependencies. The mother sums spending from the children and includes the teenage daughter's clothing allowance and the young son's extra spending. The father sums incomes from everyone, and expenses from the mother and himself.

The individual members of the family all wanted to have their own spreadsheets so they could control their own finances. The family agreed to split up the entertainment into equal parts, to divide the clothing allowance unevenly among the mother, father, and son, and to establish individual submodels for each person.

Strong

FAMILY INDIVIDUAL FINANCE   15 July 1600   B. Bunting
(C) Copyright 1986 by John M. Nevison

Give each member of the family a submodel for each individual's budget.

Contents: (each section is a named range)
INTRO	Introduction: Title, description, contents, and map.
INITIAL	Initial data and beginning assumptions
SON	Son's submodel
DAUGHTER	Daughter's submodel
MOTHER	Mother's submodel
FATHER	Father's submodel
FAMILY	Family's summary submodel
VERIFY	Verify area

Son's submodel
SON'S INITIAL AND ENTERING DATA

      20%   Son's portion of clothing allowance
            (daughter excluded from allowance)
      50%   Percent of Son's earnings he must save

		Springtime		
	April	May	June	
Outside income	0	0	18	
Allowance	5	5	5	

SON'S ENTERING DATA (FROM FATHER)

	April	May	June
Entertainment budget	15	15	17

SON'S ENTERING DATA (FROM MOTHER)

	April	May	June
Clothing budget	100	100	100

SON'S BUDGET

		Springtime		
	April	May	June	Totals
Outside income	0	0	18	18
Spending				
Entertainment	15	15	17	47
Allowance	5	5	5	15
Clothing allowance	20	20	20	60
Extra spending	0	0	9	9
Total	40	40	51	131
Saving	0	0	9	9

Daughter's submodel
DAUGHTER'S INITIAL AND ENTERING DATA

	33%	Percent of Daughter's earnings that may be spent on clothes		
			Springtime	
	April	May	June	
Outside income	100	74	130	
Allowance	15	15	15	

DAUGHTER'S ENTERING DATA (FROM FATHER)

	April	May	June	
Entertainment budget	15	15	17	

DAUGHTER'S BUDGET

		Springtime		
	April	May	June	Totals
Outside income	100	74	130	304
Spending				
Entertainment	15	15	17	47
Allowance	15	15	15	45
Clothing allowance	33	24	43	100
Total	63	54	75	192
Saving	67	50	87	204

Mother's submodel
MOTHER'S INITIAL AND ENTERING DATA

45%	Mother's portion of clothing allowance	
5%	Percent of income permitted as parent allowance	

	Springtime		
	April	May	June
Outside income	1000	1100	1200
Health ins	300	300	300
Car expenses	200	250	275
Food	200	200	200
Family clothing budget	100	100	100

MOTHER'S ENTERING DATA (FROM FATHER)

	April	May	June
Entertainment	15	15	17

MOTHER'S ENTERING DATA (FROM SON)

	April	May	June
Total spending	40	40	51

MOTHER'S ENTERING DATA (FROM DAUGHTER)

	April	May	June
Total spending	63	54	75

MOTHER'S BUDGET	Springtime			
	April	May	June	Total
Outside income	1000	1100	1200	3300
Spending				
Health ins	300	300	300	900
Car expenses	200	250	275	725
Food	200	200	200	600
Clothing allowance	45	45	45	135
Allowance at %	50	55	60	165
Entertainment	15	15	17	47
Total	810	865	897	2572
Saving	190	235	303	728
Other				
Children's spending	103	94	126	323

Father's submodel

FATHER'S INITIAL AND ENTERING DATA

35%	Father's portion of clothing allowance
3%	Percent of joint parent income for entertainment
4	Number of individuals sharing the entertainment budget
5%	Percent of income permitted as parent allowance

	Springtime		
	April	May	June
Outside income	1000	900	1050
House	450	450	450
Fuel	200	0	0
Insurance	0	0	250

FATHER'S ENTERING DATA (FROM MOTHER)

Income	1000	1100	1200
Clothing	100	100	100

FATHER'S BUDGET

	Springtime			
	April	May	June	Total
Family entertainment	60	60	67	187
Outside income	1000	900	1050	2950
Spending				
House	450	450	450	1350
Fuel	200	0	0	200
Insurance	0	0	250	250
Allowance	50	45	52	147
Entertainment	15	15	17	47
Clothing allowance	35	35	35	105
Total	750	545	804	2099
Saving	250	355	246	851

Family's summary submodel

FAMILY'S ENTERING DATA (FROM SON)   Springtime

	April	May	June
Income	0	0	18
Spending	40	40	51

FAMILY'S ENTERING DATA (FROM DAUGHTER)

Income	100	74	130
Spending	63	54	75

FAMILY'S ENTERING DATA (FROM MOTHER)

Income	1000	1100	1200
Spending	810	865	897

FAMILY'S ENTERING DATA (FROM FATHER)

Income	1000	900	1050
Spending	750	545	804

FAMILY SUMMARY BUDGET   Springtime

	April	May	June	Total
Total family income	2100	2074	2398	6572
Total family spending	1663	1504	1827	4994
Total family saving	437	570	571	1578

Verify Area

3478.43	Model verification sum
18	Son's outside income total
304	Daughter's outside income total
728.125	Mother's total saving
850.625	Father's total savings
1577.68	Total family saving

While both of these examples basically do the same thing, the spreadsheet broken into submodels is clearly easier to use in pieces. The individual submodels allow each member of the family to control his or her own portion of the model. Note that whenever any one member corrects or changes his or her submodel, the other members of the family benefit from this change—everyone's submodel is revised to reflect the latest information.

The family and its individual members are here a metaphor for any organization that has divided its work into different, semiautonomous tasks. Such tasks need to be handled a piece at a time. The corrections in one portion should be shared by all, and can be if each task is a submodel. The organization's results will be the integrated combination of all the pieces.

In the next strong example, NEWBUD, any of the submodels can be broken out and turned over to the appropriate manager to work with. The president would get the executive budget; the vice president manufacturing, the factory budget; the vice president sales, the sales budget; the vice president finance, the cash budget; the chairman of the board, the income statement and balance sheet. After each had worked over his or her individual initial and entering data, they could contribute their best estimates of their initial (but not entering) data to NEWBUD to see how the pieces fit together.

THE SUBMODEL FOCUSES ATTENTION

Different tasks imply different focuses of attention. Even if one person is responsible for all the tasks in a spreadsheet, the submodel breakdown allows that individual to focus on one area at a time. This narrowing of focus increases understanding, speeds revision, and lowers the likelihood of introducing errors in a large model. (You only have to solve that portion of the problem you are interested in. You may leave the rest neatly alone and know that it is still okay.)

Such is not the case with a large integrated model—when you change one part, you must recheck it all to assure its integrity. Consider the following model composed of six major parts. The basic idea is that four operating budgets (executive, factory, sales, and cash) coordinate with each other and then feed two accounting statements (the income statement and the balance sheet).

Contrast the terse, undocumented, large, complexly interrelated, weak example called BUDGET with the same ideas broken up in manageable pieces in the strong example called NEWBUD. Ask yourself which you would choose, if your job required you to understand, use, and revise this model.

Weak

BUDGET   1 January 1500   Peter Piper
(C) Copyright 1983 John M. Nevison

Show how three operating budgets for executive office, factory and sales office, are combined to produce the operating cash budget and the annual accounting statements.

Assumptions:

50%	Percent exec. budget allocated to factory
50%	Percent exec. budget allocated to sales
$0.20	Mnfg labor $/unit
$0.37	Raw material $/unit
45	Average age of receivables (calendar days)
90	Average age of payables (calendar days)
14.5%	Annual interest rate
*	Assumption somewhere in marked budget line

EXECUTIVE BUDGET	Qtr 1	Qtr 2	Qtr 3	Qtr 4	Year
*Total	1,160	1,165	1,164	1,170	4,659

SALES DATA	Qtr 1	Qtr 2	Qtr 3	Qtr 4	Year
*Units	23,817	23,600	24,600	25,200	97,217
*Price	1.15	1.18	1.19	1.21	

SALES BUDGET					
Revenue	27,390	27,848	29,274	30,492	115,004
Factory costs	16,417	16,621	16,656	16,530	66,224
*Delivery	80	83	86	84	333
Gross margin	10,893	11,144	12,532	13,878	48,446
*Sales support	1,350	1,400	1,430	1,487	5,667
*Advertising	90	100	110	100	400
*Selling and management	4,740	4,745	4,752	4,763	19,000
Allocated corp. overhead	580	582	582	585	2,330
Contribution	20,550	20,937	22,314	23,473	87,274

CASH BUDGET DATA

	Qtr 0	Qtr 1	Qtr 2	Qtr 3	Qtr 4	Year
*Units mfd	24,770	22,361	22,600	22,500	22,600	90,061
*Units sold	23,000	23,817	23,600	24,600	25,200	97,217
Inventory change	1,770	(1,456)	(1,000)	(2,100)	(2,600)	(7,156)
*Sales on credit	24,150	27,390	27,848	29,274	30,492	115,004
*Purchases on credit	8,424	8,334	8,423	8,386	8,423	33,568

CASH BUDGET

Receipts	Qtr 0	Qtr 1	Qtr 2	Qtr 3	Qtr 4	Year
Collected receivables		25,770	27,619	28,561	29,883	111,833
Total receipts		25,770	27,619	28,561	29,883	111,833
Disbursements						
Disbursed payables		8,424	8,334	8,423	8,386	33,568
Production payroll		4,472	4,520	4,500	4,520	18,012
Mnfing expenses		2,155	2,220	2,313	2,127	8,815
Selling expenses		6,260	6,328	6,378	6,434	25,400
Corp overhead		1,160	1,165	1,164	1,170	4,659
Interest		1,183	1,168	1,092	993	4,436
* Taxes		1,200	1,300	1,450	1,650	5,600
Total disbursements		24,854	25,035	25,321	25,280	100,490
Net cash		916	2,584	3,240	4,603	11,342
Cumulative cash						
Beginning balance		32,000	32,500	33,000	33,500	32000
Net cash		916	2,584	3,240	4,603	11,342
*Minimum balance needed		500	500	500	500	2,000
Debt reduction (increase)		416	2,084	2,740	4,103	9,342
Ending balance	32,000	32,500	33,000	33,500	34,000	34,000
Debt	32,632	32,216	30,133	27,393	23,290	23,290

ANNUAL STATEMENTS

INCOME STATEMENT	$
Sales	111,833
Cost of goods	60,395
Gross profit	51,437
Depreciation	3,500
Selling genl. & admin.	30,059
Interest	4,436
Profit before taxes	13,442
Tax	5,600
Net income	7,842

BALANCE SHEET

	Last year	Change	This year
Assets			
Current assets			
* Cash	32,000		34,000
Accounts receivable	12,075		15,246
* Raw materials	2,500		2,500
* Finished goods	8,000	(4,098)	3,902
Total current assets	54,575		55,648
Fixed assets			
* Land	2,222		2,222
* Plant and equipment	55,555		55,555
* Accumulated depreciation	11,111	3,500	14,611
Net plant and equipment	44,444		40,944
Total fixed assets	46,666		43,166
*Other assets	999		999
Total assets	102,240		99,813

Liabilities and net worth

Current liabilities			
Accounts payable	8,424		8,423
* Notes payable	12,632	(9,342)	3,290
Total current liabilities	21,056		11,713
*Long term liabilities	20,000		20,000
Common stock	35,629		40,544
*Retained earnings	25,555	2,000	27,555
Total liabilities and net worth	102,240		99,813

RATIOS

Asset turnover	1.12
Profit as a % of sales	7.0%
Return on assets	7.9%
Return on equity	11.5%

Strong

NEWBUD   2 January 1500   Peter Piper
(C) Copyright 1985 John M. Nevison

Combine three operating budgets for executive office, factory and sales office, to produce the operating cash budget, the income statement, and the balance sheet.

This spreadsheet illustrates a cooperating network of models.

For a detailed explanation of the model see Chapter Two of the following reference:
Nevison, John M., "Executive Computing: How to Get It Done With Spreadsheets and Graphs," Atlanta: GA, Association for Media-Based Continuing Education for Engineers, 1986.
Contents (Each area is a named range):

INTRODUCTION	Title, intro., contents, map, and references.
EXECUTIVE	Executive Office Budget (and initial data)
FACTORY	Factory Budget (and initial data)
SALES	Sales Budget (and initial data)
CASH	Cash Budget (and initial data)
INCOME	Income Statement (and initial data)
BALANCE	Balance Sheet (and initial data)
RATIOS	Financial Ratios (report)

EXECUTIVE BUDGET INITIAL DATA

	Qtr 1	Qtr 2	Qtr 3	Qtr 4	
Totals	1,160	1,165	1,164	1,170	

EXECUTIVE BUDGET

	Qtr 1	Qtr 2	Qtr 3	Qtr 4	Year
Total	1,160	1,165	1,164	1,170	4,659

FACTORY BUDGET INITIAL DATA

50%	Percent exec. budget allocated to factory
$0.20	Mnfg labor $/unit
$0.37	Raw material $/unit

	Qtr 1	Qtr 2	Qtr 3	Qtr 4
Units mfd	22,361	22,600	22,500	22,600
Power, heat, light	22	22	23	23
Supervision	310	325	365	300
Insurance	23	23	25	24
Depreciation	875	875	875	875
Management	1,800	1,850	1,900	1,780

FACTORY BUDGET ASSUMPTIONS (From executive budget)

	Qtr 1	Qtr 2	Qtr 3	Qtr 4
Total executive budget	1,160	1,165	1,164	1,170

FACTORY BUDGET

	Qtr 1	Qtr 2	Qtr 3	Qtr 4	Year
Direct costs					
Mnfg labor	4,472	4,520	4,500	4,520	18,012
Raw materials	8,334	8,423	8,386	8,423	33,568
Power, heat, light	22	22	23	23	90
Total direct costs	12,829	12,965	12,909	12,966	51,670
Period costs					
Supervision	310	325	365	300	1,300
Insurance	23	23	25	24	95
Depreciation	875	875	875	875	3,500
Management	1,800	1,850	1,900	1,780	7,330
Allocated corp. overhead	580	582	582	585	2,330
Total period costs	3,588	3,656	3,747	3,564	14,554
Total costs	16,417	16,621	16,656	16,530	66,224

SALES DATA INITIAL DATA

50% Percent exec. budget allocated to sales

	Qtr 1	Qtr 2	Qtr 3	Qtr 4
Units sold	23,817	23,600	24,600	25,200
Price	1.15	1.18	1.19	1.21
Delivery	80	83	86	84
Sales support	1,350	1,400	1,430	1,487
Advertising	90	100	110	100
Selling and management	4,740	4,745	4,752	4,763

SALES DATA ASSUMPTIONS (From executive budget)

	Qtr 1	Qtr 2	Qtr 3	Qtr 4
Total executive budget	1,160	1,165	1,164	1,170

SALES DATA ASSUMPTIONS (From factory budget)

	Qtr 1	Qtr 2	Qtr 3	Qtr 4
Total factory costs	16,417	16,621	16,656	16,530

SALES BUDGET	Qtr 1	Qtr 2	Qtr 3	Qtr 4	Year
Revenue	27,390	27,848	29,274	30,492	115,004
Factory costs	16,417	16,621	16,656	16,530	66,224
Delivery	80	83	86	84	333
Gross margin	10,893	11,144	12,532	13,878	48,446
Sales support	1,350	1,400	1,430	1,487	5,667
Advertising	90	100	110	100	400
Selling and management	4,740	4,745	4,752	4,763	19,000
Allocated corp. overhead	580	582	582	585	2,330
Contribution	4,133	4,317	5,658	6,943	21,050

CASH BUDGET INITIAL DATA

45	Average age of receivables (calendar days)	
90	Average age of payables (calendar days)	
14.5%	Annual interest rate	

	Qtr 0	Qtr 1	Qtr 2	Qtr 3	Qtr 4
Units mfd	24,770				
Units sold	23,000				
Sales on credit	24,150				
Purchases on credit	8,424				
Taxes		1,200	1,300	1,450	1,650
Minimum balance needed		500	500	500	500

CASH BUDGET ASSUMPTIONS (From executive budget)

		Qtr 1	Qtr 2	Qtr 3	Qtr 4
Total exec budget		1,160	1,165	1,164	1,170

CASH BUDGET ASSUMPTIONS (From factory budget)

	Qtr 1	Qtr 2	Qtr 3	Qtr 4
Units mfd	22,361	22,600	22,500	22,600
Purchases on credit	8,334	8,423	8,386	8,423
Mnfg labor	4,472	4,520	4,500	4,520
Power, heat, light	22	22	23	23
Supervision	310	325	365	300
Insurance	23	23	25	24
Management	1,800	1,850	1,900	1,780

CASH BUDGET ASSUMPTIONS (From sales budget)

	Qtr 1	Qtr 2	Qtr 3	Qtr 4
Units sold	23,817	23,600	24,600	25,200
Sales on credit	27,390	27,848	29,274	30,492
Delivery	80	83	86	84
Sales support	1,350	1,400	1,430	1,487
Advertising	90	100	110	100
Selling and management	4,740	4,745	4,752	4,763

CASH BUDGET ASSUMPTIONS (From last year's balance sheet)

Cash	32,000
Notes payable	12,632
Long term liabilities	20,000

CASH BUDGET
Tricky formulas:
 Collected receivables = (Avg age of rec./90) * last qtr sales +
                         (90 − Avg age of rec.)/90 * curr qtr sales
 Dispersed payables = (Avg age of pay./90) * last qtr sales +
                      (90 − Avg age of pay.)/90 * curr qtr sales
 Mnfing expenses = Power heat and light + supervision + insurance + management
 Selling expenses = Delivery + sales support + advertising + selling and mgt
 Interest = Annual int rate/4 * prior qtr's debt
 Cash ending balance = Beginning balance + net cash − debt reduction
 Debt = Prior qtr's debt − debt reduction

	Qtr 0	Qtr 1	Qtr 2	Qtr 3	Qtr 4	Year
Inventory change—units	1,770	(1,456)	(1,000)	(2,100)	(2,600)	(7,156)
Receipts						
Collected receivables		25,770	27,619	28,561	29,883	111,833
Total receipts		25,770	27,619	28,561	29,883	111,833
Disbursements						
Disbursed payables		8,424	8,334	8,423	8,386	33,568
Production payroll		4,472	4,520	4,500	4,520	18,012
Mnfing expenses		2,155	2,220	2,313	2,127	8,815
Selling expenses		6,260	6,328	6,378	6,434	25,400
Corp overhead		1,160	1,165	1,164	1,170	4,659
Interest		1,183	1,168	1,092	993	4,436
Taxes		1,200	1,300	1,450	1,650	5,600
Total disbursements		24,854	25,035	25,321	25,280	100,490
Net cash		916	2,584	3,240	4,603	11,342
Cumulative cash						
Beginning balance		32,000	32,500	33,000	33,500	32,000
Net cash		916	2,584	3,240	4,603	11,342
Minimum balance needed		500	500	500	500	2,000
Debt reduction (increase)		416	2,084	2,740	4,103	9,342
Ending balance	32,000	32,500	33,000	33,500	34,000	34,000
Debt	32,632	32,216	30,133	27,393	23,290	23,290

INCOME STATEMENT ASSUMPTIONS (From executive budget)

4,659	Total executive budget (corporate overhead)

INCOME STATEMENT ASSUMPTIONS (From factory budget)

3,500	Total depreciation
2,330	Total corp overhead allocated
66,224	Total costs

INCOME STATEMENT ASSUMPTIONS (From sales budget)

115,004	Total revenue
333	Total delivery costs
5,667	Total sales support costs
400	Total advertising costs
19,000	Total selling and management costs

INCOME STATEMENT ASSUMPTIONS (From cash budget)

4,436	Total interest
5,600	Total tax

INCOME STATEMENT

Tricky formulas:

 Cost of goods sold = Factory budget costs (less depreciation and corporate overhead)

 Selling, general and administrative = All the sales budget costs and the executive budget

	$	% of Sales
Sales	115,004	100.0%
Cost of goods	60,395	52.5%
Gross profit	54,609	47.5%
Depreciation	3,500	3.0%
Selling genl. & admin.	30,059	26.1%
Interest	4,436	3.9%
Profit before taxes	16,614	14.4%
Tax	5,600	4.9%
Net income	11,014	9.6%

BALANCE SHEET INITIAL DATA

Last year

32,000	Cash
2,500	Raw materials
8,000	Finished goods
2,222	Land
55,555	Plant and equipment
11,111	Accumulated depreciation
999	Other assets
12,632	Notes payable
20,000	Long term liabilities
25,555	Retained earnings
2,000	Increase (decrease) in retained earnings last year to this year

BALANCE SHEET ASSUMPTIONS (From factory budget)

$0.20	Mnfg labor $/unit
$0.37	Raw material $/unit
8,423	Qtr 4 raw material (purchases on credit)
3,500	Total depreciation

BALANCE SHEET ASSUMPTIONS (From sales budget)

30,492	Qtr 4 revenue (sales on credit)

BALANCE SHEET ASSUMPTIONS (From cash budget)

45	Average age of receivables (calendar days)
90	Average age of payables (calendar days)
8,424	Qtr 0 raw material (purchases on credit)
24,150	Qtr 0 revenue (sales on credit)
(7,156)	Total inventory change—units
9,342	Debt reduction (increase)
34,000	Ending balance of cumulative cash

BALANCE SHEET

Tricky formulas:

Cash (this year) = from accumulated cash budget

Accounts receivable = Average age of receivables/90 * 0th or 4th qtr sales on credit

Change in finished goods = change in inventory units from cash budget *
(raw mat cost/unit + mfg labor cost/unit)

Change in depreciation = from factory budget

Accounts payable = Average age of payables/90 * 0th or 4th qtr purchases on credit

Change in notes payable = from cash budget debt reduction

Change in retained earnings = from assumptions

Common stock (this year) = Total assets − short and long term liabilities − retained earnings

BALANCE SHEET

Assets	Last year	Change	This year
Current assets			
Cash	32,000		34,000
Accounts receivable	12,075		15,246
Raw materials	2,500		2,500
Finished goods	8,000	(4,098)	3,902
Total current assets	54,575		55,648
Fixed assets			
Land	2,222		2,222
Plant and equipment	55,555		55,555
Accumulated depreciation	11,111	3,500	14,611
Net plant and equipment	44,444		40,944
Total fixed assets	46,666		43,166
Other assets	999		999
Total assets	102,240		99,813

Liabilities and net worth

Current liabilities			
Accounts payable	8,424		8,423
Notes payable	12,632	(9,342)	3,290
Total current liabilities	21,056		11,713
Long term liabilities	20,000		20,000
Common stock	35,629		40,544
Retained earnings	25,555	2,000	27,555
Total liabilities and net worth	102,240		99,813

RATIOS ASSUMPTIONS FROM INCOME STATEMENT

115,004	Sales
11,014	Net income

RATIOS ASSUMPTIONS FROM BALANCE SHEET

55,648	Total assets
40,544	Common stock
27,555	Retained earnings

RATIOS (Report from income statement and balance sheet)
20-Jan-86

Corporate Financial Ratios		Formula is:
Asset turnover	2.07	Sales/total assets
Profit as a % of sales	9.6%	Net income/Sales
Return on assets	19.8%	Net income/total assets
Return on equity	16.2%	Net income/(Common stock + retained earnings)

The strong version of this model, NEWBUD, gives you, the reader, much more to work with. If you ever really wanted to understand what was going on in this model, you would study NEWBUD, not BUDGET. NEWBUD's biggest distinction is that it gives you a chance to learn one section at a time. You can understand and use one section without having mastered all of the other sections. Submodels give you intellectual control.

COLLECTIONS OF SPREADSHEETS

The cooperative effort shown here on one spreadsheet is also possible among several spreadsheets. The same Initial and Entering Data Area makes possible the coordinated use of several sheets. As the number of spreadsheets grows, the need for organization and documentation grows faster. When several spreadsheets are involved, you need a piece of paper with a picture of the whole system and directions on how to use your portion of it. To the greatest extent possible, you should include the documentation in the cooperating models themselves. (These issues will be discussed further in Chapter 6.)

CONCLUSION

Beyond the basic spreadsheet model, giving new functions new forms leads to an expanded set of areas. The areas illustrated in this book are the most common, but you should not stop here. Create your own when you need to. The concluding example in this chapter, FULL RULE, contains all the areas and lists all the rules in each area.

Strong

FULL RULE 17 July 1386 Mother Goose		Import area
TITLE TO TELL		XXXXXXX
(C) Copyright 1986 by John M. Nevison		IMPORT WITH CARE
MAKE A FORMAL INTRODUCTION		
Provide a framework with which to begin building models.		
DECLARE THE MODEL'S PURPOSE		
To use: call it up, change its name, save it with its new name, and edit to your purpose.		
GIVE CLEAR INSTRUCTIONS		
REFERENCE CRITICAL IDEAS		
Contents:	(each section is a named range)	
INTRO	Introduction: Title, description, contents.	IMPORT Import area
INITIAL	Initial data and beginning assumptions	
MODEL	Model	
REPORT	Report area	
GRAPH	Graph area	
VERIFY	Verify area	
ACTIVE	Active area	
MACRO	Macro area	
SUBMOD	Sample submodel	
MAP THE CONTENTS		

Initial data and beginning assumptions
       IDENTIFY THE DATA
       SURFACE AND LABEL EVERY ASSUMPTION

Model
       MODEL TO EXPLAIN
       POINT TO THE RIGHT SOURCE

       FIRST DESIGN ON PAPER
       TEST AND EDIT
       KEEP IT VISIBLE
       SPACE SO THE SPREADSHEET MAY BE EASILY READ
       GIVE A NEW FUNCTION A NEW AREA

Report area
       REPORT TO YOUR READER

Graph area
       GRAPH TO ILLUMINATE

Verify area
       VERIFY CRITICAL WORK

Active area
       FOCUS THE MODEL'S ACTIVITY

Macro area
       CONTROL ALL MACROS

Submodel's Initial and Entering Data area
       ENTER CAREFULLY
  Initial data
  Entering data from another submodel

Submodel

If you begin your spreadsheets with FULL RULE, you will be unlikely to commit a sin of omission: the template will remind you of most areas. You will also find that you have a quick reminder of the rules in front of you. With these rules you should be able to cover the various contingencies of spreadsheet modeling.

5

EXAMPLES

IF WISHES WERE HORSES

If wishes were horses, beggars would ride.
If turnips were watches, I would wear one by my side.
And if ''ifs'' and ''ands''
Were pots and pans,
There'd be no work for tinkers!

The proof of the rules is in their use. The first question to answer is, "How do the rules feel when you use them to build a real spreadsheet?" The second question is, "What can a finished spreadsheet say about the rules?"

THE WORKED MODEL "PROGRESS"

To see how our rules work in practice, let's work through an example from initial idea to final program. We will make notes as we go, trying to see how the rules in practice can speed the development of a structured spreadsheet.

The beginning of this spreadsheet is the template FULL RULE. We choose this template because it contains all the rules and we want them to remind us to do the right thing.

The first thing we need is a temporary name for this model. What we want to do is develop a model that contains a practical layout of a departmental budget, so we decide to call this model DEPARTMENT. We save a copy of the template under this new name.

DEPARTMENT   23 October 1986 John M. Nevison

After the new name we say out loud what we have only half thought out: "The purpose of this model is . . . ." We write down our answer and stare at the result for a few minutes, decide that it is a full order, but reasonable at this stage. We correct the spelling errors and erase the rules MAKE A FORMAL INTRODUCTION (that's ensured by the structure of the introduction area in the template), TITLE TO TELL (the title could probably be improved—let's keep alert to that possibility as we work), and DECLARE THE MODEL'S PURPOSE (just finished doing the first draft of that).

The purpose of this model is to illustrate a well-made spreadsheet that provides a department manager with the tools he needs to manage his departmental budget. In particular:

A twelve month plan for the year
A month by month list of the actual figures as they occur
Reports and graphs for the manager
Reports and graphs to be posted for the department to see
Reports and graphs for upper management

This statement of purpose begs the issue of what the reports and graphs actually are, but does alert us to the necessity of getting a clear picture of what they should be before we invest a great deal of time entering data into this model. We decide to begin with a simple list of reports in the report area and graphs in the graph area. We hope that if we choose explicit titles for these reports, we can then sketch them on a piece of paper or sketch them into the spreadsheet. If we know what some (not necessarily all) of the results are, we can then work back to the initial data and be reasonably sure that we won't forget a major item. *We design backwards, from desired results to necessary initial conditions.*

Report area
   REPORT TO YOUR READER
Departmental Quarterly Goals—public
Departmental Totals Sales, Costs, Profits Budgeted versus Actual—public
Departmental Detailed costs, Budgeted versus Actual—Dept manager
Sales and selling costs—Dept manager
Departmental YTD Profit Performance, Budgeted, Actual, Forecast—upper management

Graph area

GRAPH TO ILLUMINATE

Departmental Quarterly Sales Goal progress to date line chart—public

Departmental Totals. Sales, Costs, Profits Budgeted versus Actual—YTD each month bar chart

Sales and selling costs—Dept manager

Departmental YTD Profit Performance, Budgeted, Actual, Forecast—line chart on profit

---

The intended reader is included with the title of the reports and graphs in order to sharpen the focus of what should be included. This list makes it possible for us to rough out some reports and sketch some graphs. At this point we're beginning to feel some discomfort because we want to have fun with the spreadsheet model itself. Our better self, however, tells us first to refine what we think we want in each report and graph. (FIRST DESIGN ON PAPER.)

Designing the reports takes longer than we thought they would (about three hours). We find that we spend a great deal of time thinking through the best way to REPORT TO YOUR READER. We vary column widths. We change and rearrange rows (and columns). We format the column headings to the right side of the cells. We format the pseudo numbers and ask and re-ask if the current report is the best one for the reader. We quit working on the reports when we feel that we must know more about the actual values of the numbers to improve our thinking about the report formats.

Department goals for the quarter

OUR DEPARTMENT'S QUARTERLY PERFORMANCE
FOR MONTH OF MAY (Month 2 of Quarter 2)

	Actual	Qtrly goal	Miles to go	Rate so far	Comment
Sales	xxx.xxx	xxx.xxx	xxx.xxx	xx%	The the the
Costs	xxx.xxx	xxx.xxx	xxx.xxx	xx%	The the the
Profits	xxx.xxx	xxx.xxx	xxx.xxx	xx%	The the the

Department's year-to-date performance

OUR DEPARTMENT'S YEAR-TO-DATE PERFORMANCE
FOR MONTH OF MAY (Month 5 of 12)

	Actual	Budgeted	Rate so far	Forecast *	Rate so far	Remain...
Sales	xxx.xxx	xxx.xxx	xx%	xxx.xxx	xx%	x...
Costs	xxx.xxx	xxx.xxx	xx%	xxx.xxx	xx%	x...
Profits	xxx.xxx	xxx.xxx	xx%	xxx.xxx	xx%	x...

*Forecast is Revision of Budget

Department cost analysis

DEPARTMENTAL COST ANALYSIS
FOR MONTH OF MAY (Month 2 of Quarter 2)

	Month	Budget/for	Difference	Qtr	Budget/for	Difference
Item	xxx.xxx	xxx.xxx	xxx.xxx	xxx.xxx	xxx.xxx	xx
Item	xxx.xxx	xxx.xxx	xxx.xxx	xxx.xxx	xxx.xxx	xx
Item	xxx.xxx	xxx.xxx	xxx.xxx	xxx.xxx	xxx.xxx	xx
Item	xxx.xxx	xxx.xxx	xxx.xxx	xxx.xxx	xxx.xxx	xx
Item	xxx.xxx	xxx.xxx	xxx.xxx	xxx.xxx	xxx.xxx	xx
Total	xxx.xxx	xxx.xxx	xxx.xxx	xxx.xxx	xxx.xxx	xx

Sales and selling costs

SALES AND SELLING COSTS

	January	February	March	April	May	June
Sales	xxx.xxx	xxx.xxx	xxx.xxx	xxx.xxx	xxx.xxx	x...
Costs	xxx.xxx	xxx.xxx	xxx.xxx	xxx.xxx	xxx.xxx	x...
% of sales	xx%	xx%	xx%	xx%	xx%...	
Smoothed(5 mth)						
% of sales	xx%	xx%	xx%	xx%	xx%	

Department profit performance

IDEAL DEPARTMENT YEAR-TO-DATE PROFIT PERFORMANCE

12-Jun-86	YTD Budget	YTD Actual	Rate	Annual Budget	Annual Forecast
Sales	xxx.xxx	xxx.xxx	xx%	xxx.xxx	xxx.xxx
Variable costs	xxx.xxx	xxx.xxx	xx%	xxx.xxx	xxx.xxx
Fixed costs	xxx.xxx	xxx.xxx	xx%	xxx.xxx	xxx.xxx
Profit	xxx.xxx	xxx.xxx	xx%	xxx.xxx	xxx.xxx

The worst thing about these reports is that we know that we may change their format later. We have, however, achieved what we came for: a sharpened sense of exactly what data we will need and what the main model will look like.

To be sure we know what the results look like on paper, we print a full copy of the reports. (TEST AND EDIT.) The printed versions reveal a few minor items that we want to add, but basically confirm that these are the desired reports.

After finishing the review of the paper copy of the reports, we sketch on paper what the graphs might look like and capture the outcome of that work with some notes in the graphing area.

Graph area
GRAPH TO ILLUMINATE
Departmental Quarterly Goals: Sales, Costs, Profits. Public three pairs of bar charts.
Sales and selling costs. Rough and smooth line chart. Last 12 months
Departmental Profit Performance. Budgeted, Actual, Current Forecast—line
   chart on profits—upper management.

What we learn is that we need fewer graphs than we had thought. The selling efficiency graph, however, will require more data than only the current year: it will require thirteen months of back data.

Now a first draft of the outcomes of the spreadsheet has been completed. (Note that we hope to serve several constituencies with one spreadsheet because we know that one model can spawn several reports, each with its own report area.) We are ready to go back to the basic model and the departmental data we need to feed the model. Elapsed time at this point is four hours.

In the model itself we decide we want to see several measures at once, monthly, quarterly, half-year, and yearly. These measures will allow the department manager to pick and choose good features for quick reports on the department's performance. (If the quarterly performance is poor, the half-year figures can be emphasized.)

After an hour or so of varying the structure, we decide that we will define the "plan" to be the original budget plus periodic reforecasts to year end. Plan is the best current guess at anticipated performance. In the present case, with only one reforecast made in June, the plan is the Jan-May Budget and the June-December Forecast. If a second reforecast were made in September, the plan would have three legs: January-May, June-September, and October-December. Because the manager will want to see how close performance is to anticipated performance, the six areas necessary are:

Monthly plan
Monthly actual
Monthly difference
Summary plan
Summary actual
Summary difference

With these six sections the manager can illustrate in a few pages how the business performs. The manager can use the model areas at once, and later adjust the report areas to generate the proper month's reports and graphs.

Next we turn to the Initial Data Area to enter the data necessary to make the model real. We begin with the historical sales data because we know the model will need it to make one of the desired graphs. Then we put in the budget, the actuals to date, and the plan (which is composed of original budget numbers and later forecasts for the remainder of the year).

Initial data and beginning assumptions
May :Current month

BACK DATA	Jan.	Feb.	Mar.	Apr.	May	June	July	Aug.	Sept.	Oct.
Sales 84	12	17	19	23	22	19	18	15	18	20
Sales 85	15	17	21	27	25	20	19	14	20	20
Cost of selling 84	5.5	5.5	5.5	6.0	6.0	6.0	5.5	5.5	5.5	5.5
Cost of selling 85	5.5	5.5	5.5	5.5	5.5	5.5	5.5	5.5	5.5	5.5

ORIGINAL BUDGET	Jan.	Feb.	Mar.	Apr.	May	June	July	Aug.	Sept.	Oct.
Sales	16.0	19.0	23.0	30.0	28.0	22.0	21.0	15.0	22.0	24.0
Delivery costs	0.5	0.6	0.7	0.9	0.8	0.6	0.4	0.4	0.7	0.7
Raw material	2.4	2.8	3.4	4.5	4.2	3.3	3.0	2.2	3.3	3.6
Mfng costs	1.9	2.3	2.8	3.6	3.4	2.6	2.5	1.8	2.6	2.9
Cost of selling	5.5	5.5	5.5	6.0	6.0	5.5	5.5	5.5	5.5	5.5
Plant costs	1.0	1.0	1.0	1.0	1.0	1.0	1.0	1.0	1.0	1.0
Office costs	0.6	0.6	0.6	0.6	0.6	0.6	0.6	0.6	0.6	0.6
Admin salaries	4.0	4.0	4.0	4.0	4.0	4.0	4.0	4.0	4.0	4.0
Profit	0.1	2.2	5	9.4	8	4.4	4	−0.5	4.3	5.7

ACTUAL	Jan.	Feb.	Mar.	Apr.	May	June	July	Aug.	Sept.	Oct.
Sales	16.0	20.0	21.0	27.0	27.0	0.0	0.0	0.0	0.0	0.0
Delivery costs	0.5	0.6	0.6	0.8	0.7	0.0	0.0	0.0	0.0	0.0
Raw material	2.4	2.9	3.0	4.1	4.1	0.0	0.0	0.0	0.0	0.0
Mfng costs	1.9	2.3	2.5	3.3	3.3	0.0	0.0	0.0	0.0	0.0
Cost of selling	5.5	5.5	5.5	6.0	6.0	0.0	0.0	0.0	0.0	0.0
Plant costs	1.0	1.0	1.0	1.0	1.0	0.0	0.0	0.0	0.0	0.0
Office costs	0.6	0.6	0.6	0.6	0.6	0.0	0.0	0.0	0.0	0.0
Admin salaries	4.0	4.0	4.0	4.0	4.0	0.0	0.0	0.0	0.0	0.0

Plan is a combination of budget and on-going reforecasts (6/86)

PLAN	Jan.	Feb.	Mar.	Apr.	May	June	July	Aug.	Sept.	Oct.
Sales	16.0	19.0	23.0	30.0	28.0	21.0	20.0	14.0	21.0	23.0
Delivery costs	0.5	0.6	0.7	0.9	0.8	0.5	0.3	0.3	0.6	0.6
Raw material	2.4	2.8	3.4	4.5	4.2	3.1	2.8	2.0	3.1	3.4
Mfng costs	1.9	2.3	2.8	3.6	3.4	2.5	2.4	1.7	2.5	2.8
Cost of selling	5.5	5.5	5.5	6.0	6.0	5.5	5.5	5.5	5.5	5.5
Plant costs	1.0	1.0	1.0	1.0	1.0	1.0	1.0	1.0	1.0	1.0
Office costs	0.6	0.6	0.6	0.6	0.6	0.6	0.6	0.6	0.6	0.6
Admin salaries	4.0	4.0	4.0	4.0	4.0	4.0	4.0	4.0	4.0	4.0

After entering the data we spend a great deal of time on the model itself. The model is really the working report—the one the department manager will use to track the department's performance. The model spreads out the variable costs, the fixed costs, the sales, and the profits. It tracks the costs and profits as percentage of sales, so we can see how our variable costs track our variable sales.

While we only required the December figure for '84, we included the whole year to give ourselves some latitude for changing our mind when we return to the selling efficiency report and graph. We also computed a profits line for our original budget data because we will need it in our profit report. (Profits for Actual and Plan are computed in the Model Area.)

Model

MONTHLY PLAN May :Current month

	Jan.	Feb.	Mar.	Apr.	May	June	July	Aug.	Sept.	Oct.
Sales	16.0	19.0	23.0	30.0	28.0	21.0	20.0	14.0	21.0	23.0
Variable costs										
Delivery costs	0.5	0.6	0.7	0.9	0.8	0.5	0.3	0.3	0.6	0.6
Raw material	2.4	2.8	3.4	4.5	4.2	3.1	2.8	2.0	3.1	3.4
Mfng costs	1.9	2.3	2.8	3.6	3.4	2.5	2.4	1.7	2.5	2.8
Total var costs	4.8	5.7	6.9	9.0	8.4	6.1	5.5	4.0	6.2	6.8
(%)	30%	30%	30%	30%	30%	29%	28%	29%	30%	30%
Fixed costs										
Cost of selling	5.5	5.5	5.5	6.0	6.0	5.5	5.5	5.5	5.5	5.5
Plant costs	1.0	1.0	1.0	1.0	1.0	1.0	1.0	1.0	1.0	1.0
Office costs	0.6	0.6	0.6	0.6	0.6	0.6	0.6	0.6	0.6	0.6
Admin salaries	4.0	4.0	4.0	4.0	4.0	4.0	4.0	4.0	4.0	4.0
Total fix costs	11.1	11.1	11.1	11.6	11.6	11.1	11.1	11.1	11.1	11.1
(%)	69%	58%	48%	39%	41%	53%	56%	79%	53%	48%
Profit	0.1	2.2	5.0	9.4	8.0	3.8	3.4	−1.1	3.7	5.1
(%)	1%	12%	22%	31%	29%	18%	17%	−8%	17%	22%

MONTHLY ACTUAL May :Current month

	Jan.	Feb.	Mar.	Apr.	May	June	July	Aug.
Sales	16.0	20.0	21.0	27.0	27.0	0.0	0.0	0.0
Variable costs								
Delivery costs	0.5	0.6	0.6	0.8	0.7	0.0	0.0	0.0
Raw material	2.4	2.9	3.0	4.1	4.1	0.0	0.0	0.0
Mfng costs	1.9	2.3	2.5	3.3	3.3	0.0	0.0	0.0
Total var costs	4.8	5.8	6.1	8.2	8.1	0.0	0.0	0.0
(%)	30%	29%	29%	30%	30%	ERR	ERR	ERR
Fixed costs								
Cost of selling	5.5	5.5	5.5	6.0	6.0	0.0	0.0	0.0
Plant costs	1.0	1.0	1.0	1.0	1.0	0.0	0.0	0.0
Office costs	0.6	0.6	0.6	0.6	0.6	0.0	0.0	0.0
Admin salaries	4.0	4.0	4.0	4.0	4.0	0.0	0.0	0.0
Total fix costs	11.1	11.1	11.1	11.6	11.6	0.0	0.0	0.0
(%)	69%	56%	53%	43%	43%	ERR	ERR	ERR
Profit	0.1	3.1	3.8	7.2	7.3	0.0	0.0	0.0
(%)	1%	16%	18%	27%	27%	ERR	ERR	ERR

MONTHLY DIFFERENCE May :Current month

Difference = (actual − plan)/plan

	Jan.	Feb.	Mar.	Apr.	May	June	July	Aug.
Sales	0%	5%	−9%	−10%	−4%	−100%	−100%	−100%
Variable costs								
Delivery costs	0%	0%	−14%	−11%	−13%	−100%	−100%	−100%
Raw material	0%	4%	−12%	−9%	−2%	−100%	−100%	−100%
Mfng costs	0%	0%	−11%	−8%	−3%	−100%	−100%	−100%
Total var costs	0%	2%	−12%	−9%	−4%	−100%	−100%	−100%
(%)	0%	−3%	−3%	1%	0%	ERR	ERR	ERR
Fixed costs								
Cost of selling	0%	0%	0%	0%	0%	−100%	−100%	−100%
Plant costs	0%	0%	0%	0%	0%	−100%	−100%	−100%
Office costs	0%	0%	0%	0%	0%	−100%	−100%	−100%
Admin salaries	0%	0%	0%	0%	0%	−100%	−100%	−100%
Total fix costs	0%	0%	0%	0%	0%	−100%	−100%	−100%
(%)	0%	−5%	10%	11%	4%	ERR	ERR	ERR
Profit	0%	41%	−24%	−23%	−9%	−100%	−100%	−100%
(%)	0%	34%	−17%	−15%	−5%	ERR	ERR	ERR

We format our differences to highlight relative differences by using percentages rather than absolute amounts. We tell the reader how we calculate our difference with a formula: difference = (actual − plan)/plan.

We repeat the basic model for our summary figures.

SUMMARY PLAN	May :Current month						
	Qtr 1	Qtr 2	Qtr 3	Qtr 4	Half 1	Half 2	Year
Sales	58.0	79.0	55.0	74.0	137.0	129.0	266.0
Variable costs							
Delivery costs	1.8	2.2	1.3	2.1	4.0	3.4	7.4
Raw material	8.6	11.8	8.0	11.0	20.4	19.0	39.4
Mfng costs	7.0	9.5	6.5	8.8	16.5	15.3	31.8
Total var costs	17.4	23.5	15.8	21.9	40.9	37.7	78.6
(%)	30%	30%	29%	30%	30%	29%	30%
Fixed costs							
Cost of selling	16.5	17.5	16.5	17.5	34.0	34.0	68.0
Plant costs	3.0	3.0	3.0	3.0	6.0	6.0	12.0
Office costs	1.8	1.8	1.8	1.8	3.6	3.6	7.2
Admin salaries	12.0	12.0	12.0	12.0	24.0	24.0	48.0
Total fix costs	33.3	34.3	33.3	34.3	67.6	67.6	135.2
(%)	57%	43%	61%	46%	49%	52%	51%
Profit	7.3	21.2	5.9	17.8	28.5	23.7	52.2
(%)	13%	27%	11%	24%	21%	18%	20%

SUMMARY ACTUAL	May :Current month						
	Qtr 1	Qtr 2	Qtr 3	Qtr 4	Half 1	Half 2	Year
Sales	57.0	54.0	0.0	0.0	111.0	0.0	111.0
Variable costs							
Delivery costs	1.7	1.5	0.0	0.0	3.2	0.0	3.2
Raw material	8.3	8.2	0.0	0.0	16.5	0.0	16.5
Mfng costs	6.7	6.6	0.0	0.0	13.3	0.0	13.3
Total var costs	16.7	16.3	0.0	0.0	33.0	0.0	33.0
(%)	29%	30%	ERR	ERR	30%	ERR	30%
Fixed costs							
Cost of selling	16.5	12.0	0.0	0.0	28.5	0.0	28.5
Plant costs	3.0	2.0	0.0	0.0	5.0	0.0	5.0
Office costs	1.8	1.2	0.0	0.0	3.0	0.0	3.0
Admin salaries	12.0	8.0	0.0	0.0	20.0	0.0	20.0
Total fix costs	33.3	23.2	0.0	0.0	56.5	0.0	56.5
(%)	58%	43%	ERR	ERR	51%	ERR	51%
Profit	7.0	14.5	0.0	0.0	21.5	0.0	21.5
(%)	12%	27%	ERR	ERR	19%	ERR	19%

SUMMARY DIFFERENCE   May :Current month
Difference = (actual − plan)/plan

	Qtr 1	Qtr 2	Qtr 3	Qtr 4	Half 1	Half 2	Year
Sales	−2%	−32%	−100%	−100%	−19%	−100%	−58%
Variable costs							
Delivery costs	−6%	−32%	−100%	−100%	−20%	−100%	−57%
Raw material	−3%	−31%	−100%	−100%	−19%	−100%	−58%
Mfng costs	−4%	−31%	−100%	−100%	−19%	−100%	−58%
Total var costs	−4%	−31%	−100%	−100%	−19%	−100%	−58%
(%)	−2%	1%	ERR	ERR	0%	ERR	1%
Fixed costs							
Cost of selling	0%	−31%	−100%	−100%	−16%	−100%	−58%
Plant costs	0%	−33%	−100%	−100%	−17%	−100%	−58%
Office costs	0%	−33%	−100%	−100%	−17%	−100%	−58%
Admin salaries	0%	−33%	−100%	−100%	−17%	−100%	−58%
Total fix costs	0%	−32%	−100%	−100%	−16%	−100%	−58%
(%)	2%	−1%	ERR	ERR	3%	ERR	0%
Profit	−4%	−32%	−100%	−100%	−25%	−100%	−59%
(%)	−2%	0%	ERR	ERR	−7%	ERR	−1%

The error comments are left in the model because the model is intended for the working department manager only. The error comments remind the viewer that the full year is not yet complete. The model itself is instructive in its size. While not striving to become large, our model has reached a size where a printed copy is necessary to comprehend it. Our concern for the reader is vindicated: even the original author must be a reader. The model is far too large for the tiny screen of the computer.

The size of the model gets altered several times as we build the formulas. We change the global column width to be sure we can see as much as possible of the two- and three-digit numbers that we are manipulating. Column A gets stretched to accommodate the longer titles. The models take six hours to get right—total elapsed time is ten hours.

With the knowledge that the model may be subject to errors, we make a note to be sure to do a good Verify Area. But before doing that, we revisit the reports to get them finished with real data. As we work on them, we find that we must further revise our original ideas. We format the numbers in the reports to two decimal places so they will be familiar to the reader's eye.

Department goals for the quarter
-Be sure to adjust titles and formulas.

OUR DEPARTMENT'S QUARTERLY PERFORMANCE
FOR MONTH OF MAY (Month 2 of Quarter 2)

	Quarter to date			Until end of quarter			
	Plan	Actual	Rate	Plan	To go	Rate	Comment
Sales	58	54.0	93%	79.0	25.0	68%	Ahead of
Costs	40.6	39.5	97%	57.8	18.3	68%	"
Profits	17.4	14.5	83%	21.2	6.7	68%	"

Department's year-to-date performance
-Be sure to check titles and formulas for the current month.

OUR DEPARTMENT'S YEAR-TO-DATE PERFORMANCE
FOR MONTH OF MAY (Month 5 of 12)

	Year to date			Until end of year			
	Plan	Actual	Rate	Plan	To go	Rate	Comment
Sales	116.00	111.00	96%	266.00	155.00	42%	Try to ......
Costs	91.30	89.50	98%	213.84	124.34	42%	Keep........
Profits	24.70	21.50	87%	52.16	30.66	41%	Profits......

The first two reports are quite similar. They both report on the progress of the department—the progress during the quarter and the progress during the year. Both report areas need some directions in addition to the actual report. We include the directions at the top.

Department cost analysis
-Be sure to check titles and formulas for the current month.

DEPARTMENTAL COST ANALYSIS
FOR MONTH OF MAY (Month 2 of Quarter 2)

	Month	Plan	Difference	YTD	Plan	Difference	Rate	Comment
Delivery costs	0.70	0.80	−0.10	3.20	3.50	−0.30	91%	Variable
Raw material	4.10	4.20	−0.10	16.50	17.30	−0.80	95%	
Mfng costs	3.30	3.40	−0.10	13.30	14.00	−0.70	95%	
Cost of selling	6.00	6.00	0.00	28.50	28.50	0.00	100%	Fixed cost
Plant costs	1.00	1.00	0.00	5.00	5.00	0.00	100%	
Office costs	0.60	0.60	0.00	3.00	3.00	0.00	100%	
Admin salaries	4.00	4.00	0.00	20.00	20.00	0.00	100%	
Total	19.70	20.00	−0.30	89.50	91.30	−1.80	98%	Overall cost

The department manager uses this report to get a fix on his or her costs. The variable costs are down because sales are down, but the fixed costs remain stubbornly at the planned level. The directions warn the user that the formulas and the title must be changed for the next month.

Sales and selling costs
-Be sure to adjust smoothing formulas for last three actuals
-If sales are zero, then costs as a % of sales is 0%.

SALES AND SELLING COSTS, MONTH OF MAY

	Jan.	Feb.	Mar.	Apr.	May	June	July	Aug.	Sept.	Oct.
Sales	16.00	20.00	21.00	27.00	27.00	0.00	0.00	0.00	0.00	0.00
Costs	5.50	5.50	5.50	6.00	6.00	0.00	0.00	0.00	0.00	0.00
Costs as % of sales	34%	28%	26%	22%	22%	0%	0%	0%	0%	0%
Smoothed(5 mth)*										
Sales	21.4	22	22.2	25	27	0	0	0	0	0
Costs as % of sales	26%	25%	25%	24%	22%	0%	0%	0%	0%	0%

*Next to last month is smoothed over 3 months, last month is unsmoothed.

The report reassures the manager that underneath the seasonal fluctuation in sales, the cost of selling remains under 25% and may be declining. The "Costs as % of sales" formula contains an if . . . then function to print a zero when sales are zero in order to avoid some unnecessarily disturbing "error" messages in the cells of a report. Notes on important calculations are included in the report. (The report bleeds off the page to the right here and in regular use would require printing sideways or on wide paper.)

Department performance report
-Be sure to check titles and formulas for the current month.

12-Jun-86 · · · · · IDEAL DEPARTMENT, MONTH OF MAY

YTD IS JAN-MAY	YEAR-TO-DATE PERFORMANCE					REPLANNING		
	YTD Budget	YTD Plan	YTD Actual	Actual/ Plan	Actual/ Budget	Annual Budget	Annual Plan	Plan/Budget
Sales	116.00	116.00	111.00	96%	96%	273.00	266.00	97%
Variable costs	34.80	34.80	33.00	95%	95%	81.20	78.64	97%
Fixed costs	56.50	56.50	56.50	100%	100%	135.20	135.20	100%
Profit	24.70	24.70	21.50	87%	87%	56.60	52.16	92%

The performance report to top management is a bit different than originally envisioned. More information is included in less space. This repeated improvement of the final form should convince us that making a good report is harder than we are willing to admit. We should not think of a report as merely format—a report is a way to shape the information we want to convey. Notice that the reporting date is included on every report. We spent three more hours on our reports—elapsed time is now thirteen hours.

The next activity is to verify our model. We do that by introducing a yearly summary column on the monthly data and cross-checking the profit for the year against the sum of the monthly profits. We repeat this procedure at three other points in the model and at three points in our reports. Beneath the graphing area we construct a verify area to collect information from these cross checks.

Verify area

   297.16 The model verification sum

If an error appears here, check below and then the appropriate area of the model. (Be sure you have recalculated the whole model.)

  135.2 The monthly plan yearly profit
   21.5 The monthly actual yearly profit
  52.16 The summary plan yearly profit
   21.5 The summary actual yearly profit
   17.4 The qtr-to-date planned profits in
     Department goals for quarter report
   24.7 The year-to-date planned profits in
     Department's year-to-date performance report
   24.7 The year-to-date planned profits in
     Department performance report

After completing the verify area, we turn our attention to building the charts and graphs to accompany the reports. The graphs are changed several times as we build and review them. The graphs originally envisioned do not look as good as our hand sketches. They do, however, suggest other forms that might be improvements.

May progress report--on target for Qtr 2 goals!

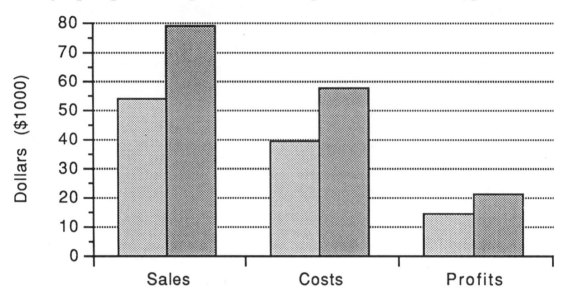

Profits follow sales, but we are a bit below plan

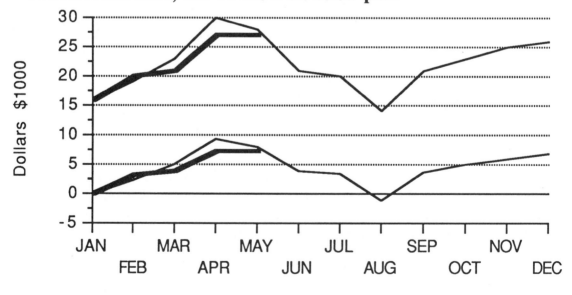

Plan and actual through May

The final charts and graphs suit the original purposes. The bar chart tells the department where it is on its way to the quarterly goals. The year-to-date sales and profit figures show how the department is performing against plan (and incidentally how all the costs are behaving, since the differences between sales and profits is costs.)

These graphs will not only be displayed for the department, they will be presented to upper management and used by the department manager. The next two charts will be used only by the department manager.

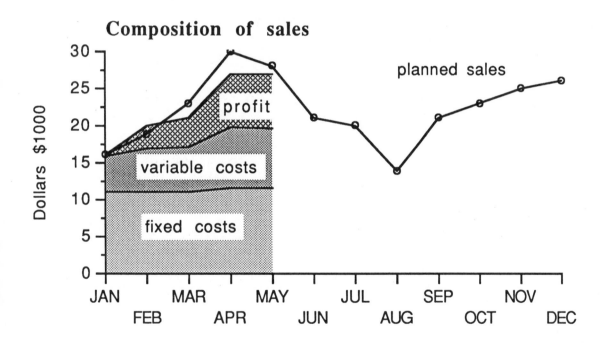

Selling efficiency improves slightly in last six months

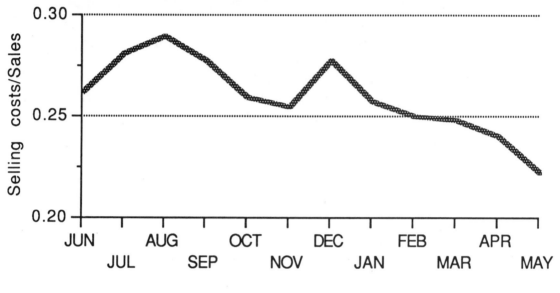

Last 12 months, current month is May

The department manager gets a look at fixed costs versus variable costs in the composition of sales chart and a look at the selling efficiency in the line chart. All graphs come with extra instructions in the appropriate graphing area. The name of each graph is also included in the graphing area.

Graph area
Qtr2 goals: Dept. Qtrly Goals, Sales, Costs, Profits—everyone

	Actual	Qtr plan
Sales	54.00	79.00
Costs	39.50	57.80
Profits	14.50	21.20

Sales and profits: planned vs. actual—everyone
Sales composition: fixed cst, var cst, profit—manager
  1. The months to come are shifted down a row to make the graph end sharply
     by using blank values (see Sales Composition graph).

	Fixed	Var	Prof	----------- Sales -----------			----------- Profit -----------		
				Budget	Plan	Actual	Budget	Plan	Actual
JAN	11.1	4.8	0.1	16.0	16.0	16.0	0.1	0.1	0.1
FEB	11.1	5.8	3.1	19.0	19.0	20.0	2.2	2.2	3.1
MAR	11.1	6.1	3.8	23.0	23.0	21.0	5.0	5.0	3.8
APR	11.6	8.2	7.2	30.0	30.0	27.0	9.4	9.4	7.2
MAY	11.6	8.1	7.3	28.0	28.0	27.0	8.0	8.0	7.3
JUN				22.0	21.0	0.0	4.4	3.8	0.0
JUL	0.0	0.0	0.0	21.0	20.0	0.0	4.0	3.4	0.0
AUG	0.0	0.0	0.0	15.0	14.0	0.0	−0.5	−1.1	0.0
SEP	0.0	0.0	0.0	22.0	21.0	0.0	4.3	3.7	0.0
OCT	0.0	0.0	0.0	24.0	23.0	0.0	5.7	5.1	0.0
NOV	0.0	0.0	0.0	26.0	25.0	0.0	6.6	6.0	0.0
DEC	0.0	0.0	0.0	27.0	26.0	0.0	7.4	6.8	0.0
	0.0	0.0	0.0						

Selling efficiency: last 12 months, cost of sales/smoothed sales (5 mth smoothing)—dept mgr
 1. Insert a blank row at the beginning of current 12 months.
 2. Change the smoothing formulas near the end of the current 12 months.
   (Next to last is 3 month, last is raw)

	Sales	Smoothed	Costs	Costs/Smoothed Sales
DEC	23.0		6.0	
JAN	15.0		5.5	
FEB	17.0	20.6	5.5	0.2670
MAR	21.0	21.0	5.5	0.2619
APR	27.0	22.0	5.5	0.2500
MAY	25.0	22.4	5.5	0.2455
JUN	20.0	21.0	5.5	0.2619
JUL	19.0	19.6	5.5	0.2806
AUG	14.0	19.0	5.5	0.2895
SEP	20.0	19.8	5.5	0.2778
OCT	22.0	21.2	5.5	0.2594
NOV	24.0	21.6	5.5	0.2546
DEC	26.0	21.6	6.0	0.2778
JAN	16.0	21.4	5.5	0.2570
FEB	20.0	22.0	5.5	0.2500
MAR	21.0	22.2	5.5	0.2477
APR	27.0	25.0**	6.0	0.2400
MAY	27.0	27.0**	6.0	0.2222
JUN	0.0		0.0	
JUL	0.0		0.0	
AUG	0.0		0.0	
SEP	0.0		0.0	
OCT	0.0		0.0	
NOV	0.0		0.0	
DEC	0.0		0.0	

**formulas need work

Our graphing area allows us to be concerned with how the user makes graphs. We mark special formulas for revision. We give special instructions where necessary. We keep the data streams compactly arranged in vertical columns.

The graphing area contains odd-looking tables that help make good-looking graphs. We shift the inactive data down one month to create a blank line that causes the graphed areas to stop cleanly. By shifting the block down a line, we preserve our formulas so we only have to do simple moving, not complicated formula rebuilding, when we move on to the next month. We can also insert a blank line to clearly mark the beginning of a rolling twelve-month selling efficiency graph.

We store numbers in a format that keeps us from making mistakes when we graph. A rate is displayed as .2895, a number visibly between zero and one, and not 29%, a number one might mistakenly try to find between one and one hundred. The graphs take four hours to complete. Our total elapsed time is seventeen hours.

We add some easy-to-follow instructions to the Introduction and feel pretty good about our completed spreadsheet. We decide to take it out for a test drive. We will add a month of June actuals and follow our instructions to see how the parts work.

To use:
1. Add new actual data.
2. Be sure to restrict reforecasts to the plan from present until year-end.
3. Adjust report formulas, and titles before printing them out.
4. Adjust graphing area and graphs before printing.
5. Print out selected models, reports, and graphs as needed.

The month of June was a good month with better-than-expected sales. We enter the data and alter the formulas. While we alter formulas, the verify warnings turn on twice to alert us that formulas do not cross check. An hour later the new spreadsheet is complete. The reports make sense. The graphs neatly summarize the information. Our test drive convinces us that the model can be used repeatedly by an informed assistant. The instructions are sound and will work in practice.

We also realize that our manager might want to play "what if?" with the model, so we include some directions on how to go about doing that.

To model various sales levels:
1. Be sure to use a renamed copy of this spreadsheet: NOT THE ORIGINAL.
2. Type in projected sales in Actual Initial Data.
3. Use a formula of your choice to project variable costs.
4. Adjust selected fixed costs (or hold constant).
5. Print out selected models, reports, and graphs as needed (Be sure to label as projections).

(One way of reducing a variable cost to a percentage of sales is:

Variable cost % of sales = <sum of costs so far>/<sum of sales so far>

With this percentage, the user can project sales and variable costs as a percentage of sales.) We decide the instructions can withstand the test of use.

We give the model to a friend to proofread. His comments are: "I liked it. I had some questions in the Initial Data, but I answered them when I read the model. The spreadsheet looks like it might be useful, and I may want to use a copy. The reports and graphs made sense."

As a final step, we protect against accidental alteration of a cell by explicitly unprotecting those cells that we wish to allow people to change. By explicitly unprotecting cells, we enforce the assumption that a cell will be protected unless a special effort was made to unprotect it.

We compare the time it took to build the model with the time it took to revise it and conclude that the twenty-hour investment will repay our efforts with swift, error-free updates each month. The time invested in writing the model well will be repaid in time not spent awkwardly modifying an error-ridden tangle of formulas and hidden constants.

Finally, four days later, a good name for the model pops into our head: PROG-RESS. The purpose of the model is to track our department's progress against its plan. We adopt our new title, polish up our statement of purpose, note our revision, and call our job done. The entire model looks like this:

PROGRESS   17 November 1986   John M. Nevison
(C) Copyright 1986 by John M. Nevison

Revision history:
21 Nov 86   JMN changed the title and rewrote the purpose statement
                 and table of contents.

The purpose of this model is to illustrate a well-made spreadsheet that
provides a department manager with the tools he needs to track his
department's budget progress against its plan. It includes:
    A twelve month plan for the year,
    A month by month list of the actual figures as they occur.
    Reports and graphs for the manager
    Reports and graphs to be posted for the department to see
    Reports and graphs for upper management

To use:

1. Add new actual data.
2. Be sure to restrict reforecasts to the plan from present until year-end.
3. Adjust report formulas, and titles before printing them out.
4. Adjust graphing area and graphs before printing.
5. Print out selected models, reports, and graphs as needed.

To model various sales levels:

1. Be sure to use a renamed copy of this spreadsheet; NOT THE ORIGINAL.
2. Type in projected sales in Actual Initial Data.
3. Use a formula of your choice to project variable costs.
4. Adjust selected fixed costs (or hold constant).
5. Print out selected models, reports, and graphs as needed (Be sure to label as projections)

Contents: (each section is a named range)

INTRO	Introduction:Title, description, contents.
INITIAL	Initial data and beginning assumptions
	Back data
	Initial budget
	Actual budget to date
	Plan (budget plus reforecasts)
MODEL	Twelve month model
	Plan
	Actual
	Difference
	Summary models: quarters, halves, year
	Plan
	Actual
	Difference
REPORT1	Department goals for quarter
REPORT2	Department's year-to-date performance
REPORT3	Department cost analysis
REPORT4	Sales and selling costs
REPORT5	Department performance report
GRAPH	Graphs:
	Qtr2 goals
	Sales and profits
	Sales composition
	Selling efficiency
VERIFY	Verify area

Initial data and beginning assumptions
May :Current month

BACK DATA	Jan.	Feb.	Mar.	Apr.	May	June	July	Aug.	Sept.	Oct.	Nov.	Dec.
Sales 84	12	17	19	23	22	19	18	15	18	20	23	23
Sales 85	15	17	21	27	25	20	19	14	20	22	24	26
Cost of selling 84	5.5	5.5	5.5	6.0	6.0	6.0	5.5	5.5	5.5	5.5	5.5	6.0
Cost of selling 85	5.5	5.5	5.5	5.5	5.5	5.5	5.5	5.5	5.5	5.5	5.5	6.0

ORIGINAL BUDGET	Jan.	Feb.	Mar.	Apr.	May	June	July	Aug.	Sept.	Oct.	Nov.	Dec.
Sales	16.0	19.0	23.0	30.0	28.0	22.0	21.0	15.0	22.0	24.0	26.0	27.0
Delivery costs	0.5	0.6	0.7	0.9	0.8	0.6	0.4	0.4	0.7	0.7	0.8	0.8
Raw material	2.4	2.8	3.4	4.5	4.2	3.3	3.0	2.2	3.3	3.6	3.9	4.0
Mfng costs	1.9	2.3	2.8	3.6	3.4	2.6	2.5	1.8	2.6	2.9	3.1	3.2
Cost of selling	5.5	5.5	5.5	6.0	6.0	5.5	5.5	5.5	5.5	5.5	6.0	6.0
Plant costs	1.0	1.0	1.0	1.0	1.0	1.0	1.0	1.0	1.0	1.0	1.0	1.0
Office costs	0.6	0.6	0.6	0.6	0.6	0.6	0.6	0.6	0.6	0.6	0.6	0.6
Admin salaries	4.0	4.0	4.0	4.0	4.0	4.0	4.0	4.0	4.0	4.0	4.0	4.0
Profit	0.1	2.2	5	9.4	8	4.4	4	−0.5	4.3	5.7	6.6	7.4

ACTUAL	Jan.	Feb.	Mar.	Apr.	May	June	July	Aug.	Sept.	Oct.	Nov.	Dec.
Sales	16.0	20.0	21.0	27.0	27.0	0.0	0.0	0.0	0.0	0.0	0.0	0.0
Delivery costs	0.5	0.6	0.6	0.8	0.7	0.0	0.0	0.0	0.0	0.0	0.0	0.0
Raw material	2.4	2.9	3.0	4.1	4.1	0.0	0.0	0.0	0.0	0.0	0.0	0.0
Mfng costs	1.9	2.3	2.5	3.3	3.3	0.0	0.0	0.0	0.0	0.0	0.0	0.0
Cost of selling	5.5	5.5	5.5	6.0	6.0	0.0	0.0	0.0	0.0	0.0	0.0	0.0
Plant costs	1.0	1.0	1.0	1.0	1.0	0.0	0.0	0.0	0.0	0.0	0.0	0.0
Office costs	0.6	0.6	0.6	0.6	0.6	0.0	0.0	0.0	0.0	0.0	0.0	0.0
Admin salaries	4.0	4.0	4.0	4.0	4.0	0.0	0.0	0.0	0.0	0.0	0.0	0.0

Plan is a combination of budget and on-going reforecasts (6/86)

PLAN	Jan.	Feb.	Mar.	Apr.	May	June	July	Aug.	Sept.	Oct.	Nov.	Dec.
Sales	16.0	19.0	23.0	30.0	28.0	21.0	20.0	14.0	21.0	23.0	25.0	26.0
Delivery costs	0.5	0.6	0.7	0.9	0.8	0.5	0.3	0.3	0.6	0.6	0.7	0.7
Raw material	2.4	2.8	3.4	4.5	4.2	3.1	2.8	2.0	3.1	3.4	3.7	3.8
Mfng costs	1.9	2.3	2.8	3.6	3.4	2.5	2.4	1.7	2.5	2.8	3.0	3.1
Cost of selling	5.5	5.5	5.5	6.0	6.0	5.5	5.5	5.5	5.5	5.5	6.0	6.0
Plant costs	1.0	1.0	1.0	1.0	1.0	1.0	1.0	1.0	1.0	1.0	1.0	1.0
Office costs	0.6	0.6	0.6	0.6	0.6	0.6	0.6	0.6	0.6	0.6	0.6	0.6
Admin salaries	4.0	4.0	4.0	4.0	4.0	4.0	4.0	4.0	4.0	4.0	4.0	4.0

Model

MONTHLY PLAN May : Current month

	Jan.	Feb.	Mar.	Apr.	May	June	July	Aug.	Sept.	Oct.	Nov.	Dec.
Sales	16.0	19.0	23.0	30.0	28.0	21.0	20.0	14.0	21.0	23.0	25.0	26.0
Variable costs												
Delivery costs	0.5	0.6	0.7	0.9	0.8	0.5	0.3	0.3	0.6	0.6	0.7	0.7
Raw material	2.4	2.8	3.4	4.5	4.2	3.1	2.8	2.0	3.1	3.4	3.7	3.8
Mfng costs	1.9	2.3	2.8	3.6	3.4	2.5	2.4	1.7	2.5	2.8	3.0	3.1
Total var costs	4.8	5.7	6.9	9.0	8.4	6.1	5.5	4.0	6.2	6.8	7.4	7.6
(%)	30%	30%	30%	30%	30%	29%	28%	29%	30%	30%	30%	29%
Fixed costs												
Cost of selling	5.5	5.5	5.5	6.0	6.0	5.5	5.5	5.5	5.5	5.5	6.0	6.0
Plant costs	1.0	1.0	1.0	1.0	1.0	1.0	1.0	1.0	1.0	1.0	1.0	1.0
Office costs	0.6	0.6	0.6	0.6	0.6	0.6	0.6	0.6	0.6	0.6	0.6	0.6
Admin salaries	4.0	4.0	4.0	4.0	4.0	4.0	4.0	4.0	4.0	4.0	4.0	4.0
Total fix costs	11.1	11.1	11.1	11.6	11.6	11.1	11.1	11.1	11.1	11.1	11.6	11.6
(%)	69%	58%	48%	39%	41%	53%	56%	79%	53%	48%	46%	45%
Profit	0.1	2.2	5.0	9.4	8.0	3.8	3.4	−1.1	3.7	5.1	6.0	6.8
(%)	1%	12%	22%	31%	29%	18%	17%	−8%	17%	22%	24%	26%

MONTHLY ACTUAL May : Current month

	Jan.	Feb.	Mar.	Apr.	May	June	July	Aug.	Sept.	Oct.	Nov.	Dec.
Sales	16.0	20.0	21.0	27.0	27.0	0.0	0.0	0.0	0.0	0.0	0.0	0.0
Variable costs												
Delivery costs	0.5	0.6	0.6	0.8	0.7	0.0	0.0	0.0	0.0	0.0	0.0	0.0
Raw material	2.4	2.9	3.0	4.1	4.1	0.0	0.0	0.0	0.0	0.0	0.0	0.0
Mfng costs	1.9	2.3	2.5	3.3	3.3	0.0	0.0	0.0	0.0	0.0	0.0	0.0
Total var costs	4.8	5.8	6.1	8.2	8.1	0.0	0.0	0.0	0.0	0.0	0.0	0.0
(%)	30%	29%	29%	30%	30%	ERR	ERR	ERR	ERR	ERR	ERR	ERR
Fixed costs												
Cost of selling	5.5	5.5	5.5	6.0	6.0	0.0	0.0	0.0	0.0	0.0	0.0	0.0
Plant costs	1.0	1.0	1.0	1.0	1.0	0.0	0.0	0.0	0.0	0.0	0.0	0.0
Office costs	0.6	0.6	0.6	0.6	0.6	0.0	0.0	0.0	0.0	0.0	0.0	0.0
Admin salaries	4.0	4.0	4.0	4.0	4.0	0.0	0.0	0.0	0.0	0.0	0.0	0.0
Total fix costs	11.1	11.1	11.1	11.6	11.6	0.0	0.0	0.0	0.0	0.0	0.0	0.0
(%)	69%	56%	53%	43%	43%	ERR	ERR	ERR	ERR	ERR	ERR	ERR
Profit	0.1	3.1	3.8	7.2	7.3	0.0	0.0	0.0	0.0	0.0	0.0	0.0
(%)	1%	16%	18%	27%	27%	ERR	ERR	ERR	ERR	ERR	ERR	ERR

MONTHLY DIFFERENCE   May :Current month
Difference = (actual − plan)/plan

	Jan.	Feb.	Mar.	Apr.	May	June	July	Aug.	Sept.	Oct.	Nov.	Dec.
Sales	0%	5%	−9%	−10%	−4%	−100%	−100%	−100%	−100%	−100%	−100%	−100%
Variable costs												
Delivery costs	0%	0%	−14%	−11%	−13%	−100%	−100%	−100%	−100%	−100%	−100%	−100%
Raw material	0%	4%	−12%	−9%	−2%	−100%	−100%	−100%	−100%	−100%	−100%	−100%
Mfng costs	0%	0%	−11%	−8%	−3%	−100%	−100%	−100%	−100%	−100%	−100%	−100%
Total var costs	0%	2%	−12%	−9%	−4%	−100%	−100%	−100%	−100%	−100%	−100%	−100%
(%)	0%	−3%	−3%	1%	0%	ERR	ERR	ERR	ERR	ERR	ERR	ERR
Fixed costs												
Cost of selling	0%	0%	0%	0%	0%	−100%	−100%	−100%	−100%	−100%	−100%	−100%
Plant costs	0%	0%	0%	0%	0%	−100%	−100%	−100%	−100%	−100%	−100%	−100%
Office costs	0%	0%	0%	0%	0%	−100%	−100%	−100%	−100%	−100%	−100%	−100%
Admin salaries	0%	0%	0%	0%	0%	−100%	−100%	−100%	−100%	−100%	−100%	−100%
Total fix costs	0%	0%	0%	0%	0%	−100%	−100%	−100%	−100%	−100%	−100%	−100%
(%)	0%	−5%	10%	11%	4%	ERR	ERR	ERR	ERR	ERR	ERR	ERR
Profit	0%	41%	−24%	−23%	−9%	−100%	−100%	−100%	−100%	−100%	−100%	−100%
(%)	0%	34%	−17%	−15%	−5%	ERR	ERR	ERR	ERR	ERR	ERR	ERR

SUMMARY PLAN   May :Current month

	Qtr 1	Qtr 2	Qtr 3	Qtr 4	Half 1	Half 2	Year
Sales	58.0	79.0	55.0	74.0	137.0	129.0	266.0
Variable costs							
Delivery costs	1.8	2.2	1.3	2.1	4.0	3.4	7.4
Raw material	8.6	11.8	8.0	11.0	20.4	19.0	39.4
Mfng costs	7.0	9.5	6.5	8.8	16.5	15.3	31.8
Total var costs	17.4	23.5	15.8	21.9	40.9	37.7	78.6
(%)	30%	30%	29%	30%	30%	29%	30%
Fixed costs							
Cost of selling	16.5	17.5	16.5	17.5	34.0	34.0	68.0
Plant costs	3.0	3.0	3.0	3.0	6.0	6.0	12.0
Office costs	1.8	1.8	1.8	1.8	3.6	3.6	7.2
Admin salaries	12.0	12.0	12.0	12.0	24.0	24.0	48.0
Total fix costs	33.3	34.3	33.3	34.3	67.6	67.6	135.2
(%)	57%	43%	61%	46%	49%	52%	51%
Profit	7.3	21.2	5.9	17.8	28.5	23.7	52.2
(%)	13%	27%	11%	24%	21%	18%	20%

SUMMARY ACTUAL   May :Current month

	Qtr 1	Qtr 2	Qtr 3	Qtr 4	Half 1	Half 2	Year
Sales	57.0	54.0	0.0	0.0	111.0	0.0	111.0
Variable costs							
Delivery costs	1.7	1.5	0.0	0.0	3.2	0.0	3.2
Raw material	8.3	8.2	0.0	0.0	16.5	0.0	16.5
Mfng costs	6.7	6.6	0.0	0.0	13.3	0.0	13.3
Total var costs	16.7	16.3	0.0	0.0	33.0	0.0	33.0
(%)	29%	30%	ERR	ERR	30%	ERR	30%
Fixed costs							
Cost of selling	16.5	12.0	0.0	0.0	28.5	0.0	28.5
Plant costs	3.0	2.0	0.0	0.0	5.0	0.0	5.0
Office costs	1.8	1.2	0.0	0.0	3.0	0.0	3.0
Admin salaries	12.0	8.0	0.0	0.0	20.0	0.0	20.0
Total fix costs	33.3	23.2	0.0	0.0	56.5	0.0	56.5
(%)	58%	43%	ERR	ERR	51%	ERR	51%
Profit	7.0	14.5	0.0	0.0	21.5	0.0	21.5
(%)	12%	27%	ERR	ERR	19%	ERR	19%

SUMMARY DIFFERENCE   May :Current month

Difference = (actual − plan)/plan

	Qtr 1	Qtr 2	Qtr 3	Qtr 4	Half 1	Half 2	Year
Sales	−2%	−32%	−100%	−100%	−19%	−100%	−58%
Variable costs							
Delivery costs	−6%	−32%	−100%	−100%	−20%	−100%	−57%
Raw material	−3%	−31%	−100%	−100%	−19%	−100%	−58%
Mfng costs	−4%	−31%	−100%	−100%	−19%	−100%	−58%
Total var costs	−4%	−31%	−100%	−100%	−19%	−100%	−58%
(%)	−2%	1%	ERR	ERR	0%	ERR	1%
Fixed costs							
Cost of selling	0%	−31%	−100%	−100%	−16%	−100%	−58%
Plant costs	0%	−33%	−100%	−100%	−17%	−100%	−58%
Office costs	0%	−33%	−100%	−100%	−17%	−100%	−58%
Admin salaries	0%	−33%	−100%	−100%	−17%	−100%	−58%
Total fix costs	0%	−32%	−100%	−100%	−16%	−100%	−58%
(%)	2%	−1%	ERR	ERR	3%	ERR	0%
Profit	−4%	−32%	−100%	−100%	−25%	−100%	−59%
(%)	−2%	0%	ERR	ERR	−7%	ERR	−1%

Department goals for the quarter
-Be sure to adjust titles and formulas.

12-Jun-86   OUR DEPARTMENT'S QUARTERLY PERFORMANCE
FOR MONTH OF MAY (Month 2 of Quarter 2)

	Quarter to date			Until end of quarter			
	Plan	Actual	Rate	Plan	To go	Rate	Comment
Sales	58	54.0	93%	79.0	25.0	68%	Ahead of the game
Costs	40.6	39.5	97%	57.8	18.3	68%	"
Profits	17.4	14.5	83%	21.2	6.7	68%	"

Department's year-to-date performance
-Be sure to check titles and formulas for the current month.

12-Jun-86   OUR DEPARTMENT'S YEAR-TO-DATE PERFORMANCE
FOR MONTH OF MAY (Month 5 of 12)

	Year to date			Until end of year			
	Plan	Actual	Rate	Plan	To go	Rate	Comment
Sales	116.00	111.00	96%	266.00	155.00	42%	Try to recover $5
Costs	91.30	89.50	98%	213.84	124.34	42%	Keep control of costs
Profits	24.70	21.50	87%	52.16	30.66	41%	Profits down $3

Department cost analysis
-Be sure to check titles and formulas for the current month.

12-Jun-86   DEPARTMENTAL COST ANALYSIS
FOR MONTH OF MAY (Month 2 of Quarter 2)

	Month	Plan	Differ...	YTD	Plan	Differ...	Rate	Comment
Delivery costs	0.70	0.80	−0.10	3.20	3.50	−0.30	91%	Variable costs off
Raw material	4.10	4.20	−0.10	16.50	17.30	−0.80	95%	
Mfng costs	3.30	3.40	−0.10	13.30	14.00	−0.70	95%	
Cost of selling	6.00	6.00	0.00	28.50	28.50	0.00	100%	Fixed costs on target
Plant costs	1.00	1.00	0.00	5.00	5.00	0.00	100%	
Office costs	0.60	0.60	0.00	3.00	3.00	0.00	100%	
Admin salaries	4.00	4.00	0.00	20.00	20.00	0.00	100%	
Total	19.70	20.00	−0.30	89.50	91.30	−1.80	98%	Overall costs a little high

Sales and selling costs
-Be sure to adjust smoothing formulas for last three actuals
-If sales are zero, then costs as a % of sales is 0%.

12-Jun-86	Jan.	Feb.	Mar.	Apr.	May	June	July	Aug.	Sept.	Oct.
	SALES AND SELLING COSTS, MONTH OF MAY									
Sales	16.00	20.00	21.00	27.00	27.00	0.00	0.00	0.00	0.00	0.00
Costs	5.50	5.50	5.50	6.00	6.00	0.00	0.00	0.00	0.00	0.00
Costs as % of sales	34%	28%	26%	22%	22%	0%	0%	0%	0%	0%
Smoothed(5 mth)*										
Sales	21.4	22	22.2	25	27	0	0	0	0	0
Costs as % of sales	26%	25%	25%	24%	22%	0%	0%	0%	0%	0%

*Next to last month is smoothed over 3 months, last month is unsmoothed.
Note: This report is supported by the graph "Selling efficiency—last 12 months"

Department performance report
-Be sure to check titles and formulas for the current month.

12-Jun-86 IDEAL DEPARTMENT, MONTH OF MAY
YEAR-TO-DATE PERFORMANCE   REPLANNING

YTD IS JAN-MAY	YTD Budget	YTD Plan	YTD Actual	Actual/ Plan	Actual/ Budget	Annual Budget	Annual Plan	Plan/Budget
Sales	116.00	116.00	111.00	96%	96%	273.00	266.00	97%
Variable costs	34.80	34.80	33.00	95%	95%	81.20	78.64	97%
Fixed costs	56.50	56.50	56.50	100%	100%	135.20	135.20	100%
Profit	24.70	24.70	21.50	87%	87%	56.60	52.16	92%

Graph area
"Qtr2 goals": Dept. Qtrly Goals, Sales, Costs, Profits—everyone

	Actual	Qtr plan
Sales	54.00	79.00
Costs	39.50	57.80
Profits	14.50	21.20

"Sales and profits": planned vs. actual—everyone

"Sales composition": fixed cst, var cst, profit—manager

1. The months to come are shifted down a row to make the graph end sharply by using blank values (see Sales Composition graph).

	Fixed	Var	Prof	----------- Sales -----------			----------- Profit -----------		
				Budget	Plan	Actual	Budget	Plan	Actual
JAN	11.1	4.8	0.1	16.0	16.0	16.0	0.1	0.1	0.1
FEB	11.1	5.8	3.1	19.0	19.0	20.0	2.2	2.2	3.1
MAR	11.1	6.1	3.8	23.0	23.0	21.0	5.0	5.0	3.8
APR	11.6	8.2	7.2	30.0	30.0	27.0	9.4	9.4	7.2
MAY	11.6	8.1	7.3	28.0	28.0	27.0	8.0	8.0	7.3
JUN				22.0	21.0	0.0	4.4	3.8	0.0
JUL	0.0	0.0	0.0	21.0	20.0	0.0	4.0	3.4	0.0
AUG	0.0	0.0	0.0	15.0	14.0	0.0	−0.5	−1.1	0.0
SEP	0.0	0.0	0.0	22.0	21.0	0.0	4.3	3.7	0.0
OCT	0.0	0.0	0.0	24.0	23.0	0.0	5.7	5.1	0.0
NOV	0.0	0.0	0.0	26.0	25.0	0.0	6.6	6.0	0.0
DEC	0.0	0.0	0.0	27.0	26.0	0.0	7.4	6.8	0.0
	0.0	0.0	0.0						

"Selling efficiency": last 12 months, cost of sales/smoothed sales (5 mth smoothing)—dept manager
1. Insert a blank row at the beginning of current 12 months.
2. Change the smoothing formulas near the end of the current 12 months.
    (Next to last is 3 month, last is raw)

	Sales	Smoothed	Costs	Costs/Smoothed Sales
DEC	23.0		6.0	
JAN	15.0		5.5	
FEB	17.0	20.6	5.5	0.2670
MAR	21.0	21.0	5.5	0.2619
APR	27.0	22.0	5.5	0.2500
MAY	25.0	22.4	5.5	0.2455
JUN	20.0	21.0	5.5	0.2619
JUL	19.0	19.6	5.5	0.2806
AUG	14.0	19.0	5.5	0.2895
SEP	20.0	19.8	5.5	0.2778
OCT	22.0	21.2	5.5	0.2594
NOV	24.0	21.6	5.5	0.2546
DEC	26.0	21.6	6.0	0.2778
JAN	16.0	21.4	5.5	0.2570
FEB	20.0	22.0	5.5	0.2500
MAR	21.0	22.2	5.5	0.2477
APR	27.0	25.0**	6.0	0.2400
MAY	27.0	27.0**	6.0	0.2222
JUN	0.0		0.0	
JUL	0.0		0.0	
AUG	0.0		0.0	
SEP	0.0		0.0	
OCT	0.0		0.0	
NOV	0.0		0.0	
DEC	0.0		0.0	

**formulas need work

Verify area

        297.16   The model verification sum

If an error appears here, check below and then the appropriate area of the model. (Be sure you have recalculated the whole model.)

       135.2   The monthly plan yearly profit
        21.5   The monthly actual yearly profit
       52.16   The summary plan yearly profit
        21.5   The summary actual yearly profit
       17.4   The qtr-to-date planned profits in
           Departmentals goals for quarter report
       24.7   The year-to-date planned profits in
           Department's year-to-date performance report
       24.7   The year-to-date planned profits in
           Department performance report

THE MODEL "QUEST"

The next model is the complete version of QUEST. This spreadsheet helps a reader decide between alternatives evaluated with several conflicting criteria. Read in its entirety, QUEST provides a good example of what a model built for use and reuse might look like.

QUEST   15 October 1488   King Henry

Pick the best land to gain glory with a quest.

Decide which choice best satisfies several required and desired objectives.
List the choices, then list and weight the objectives to be met. Rank the choices against each other and pick the choice with the highest weighted score.

Reference: Kepner, Charles H., and Tregoe, Benjamin B., "The New Rational Manager,"
          Princeton, NJ: Princeton Research Press, 1981, pp. 83-102.

Contents: (each section is a named range)
 INTRO   Introduction: Title, description, contents, and directions.
 INITIAL Initial data and beginning assumptions
 MODEL Decision model
 GRAPH Choice's bar graph.

Directions:
In the initial data area:
1. State the decision and the desired result.
2. Put in choices and make comments.
3. Enter "must" objectives—things that must be satisfied.
4. Enter "want" objectives—things that you would like to have.
5. Weight the importance of the "want" objectives and comment.
6. Rate or rank the choices against each objective.
    For example, rate the best choice (of four) as 4 and let the others have 3, 2, or 1.
    You may have ties if you wish. You may rate a choice 0 if you wish.
In the decision model
7. Examine the model's results and graph.
8. Revise and reexamine the importance of objectives, the rank of choices, and other features to be sure of your choice.
9. List the adverse consequences of the best choice to see if it will work.

The introduction covers a lot of important ground, including a brief reference to a source which explains the full method behind the spreadsheet. The directions give step-by-step guidance to the user.

Initial data and beginning assumptions

DECISION AND RESULT:
               Pick the best land to gain glory with a quest.

CHOICES   COMMENTS
Northumberland   Nice country, lots of dwarves.
Easton   Tough country, magic rings in abundance.
Southington   No known questing beast.
Westerly   Good roads, friendly elves.

"MUST" OBJECTIVES   COMMENTS
Questing Beast   A questing beast to be slain
Maiden in distress   A maiden to be rescued
Holy relic   A relic to bring back to the Church

"WANT" OBJECTIVES   IMPORTANCE AND COMMENTS
Elves   10 Have magic, can be big help on quest
Magic rings   10 Help in the quest
Good camps   9 Water and firewood for camps
Smooth roads   7 Easy to travel
Golden treasures   5 Nice to find
Dwarves   4 Can help on the quest
Friendly castles   2 Places to stay
Trolls   1 Some help with bridges

The Initial Data Area tells quite a story. The King needs to choose which of four kingdoms to explore on a quest. He needs to bring back a holy relic, slay a questing beast, and rescue a maiden in distress. He would like to have the help of elves and magic rings. He would like good travel conditions. Of less importance to him are the presence of golden treasures, dwarves, friendly castles, and trolls.

The first part of the initial data is mostly text. Notice, however, that the names of the four lands can be data for some spreadsheets that allow pointing to a label. The most important feature about this first part of the Initial Data Area is that it provides room for the necessary information to be spread out and not only identified, but commented upon where appropriate. The most important data entered here is the relative importance given to the various criteria by which the user will evaluate the choices.

	Nort...	Easton	Southin...	Westerly
Questing Beast	1	1	0	1
Maiden in distress	1	1	1	1
Holy relic	1	1	1	0

	Relative scores			
Elves	2	2	3	4
Magic rings	1	4	1	4
Good camps	4	1	3	2
Smooth roads	1	3	2	4
Golden treasures	4	3	2	1
Dwarves	4	4	2	1
Friendly castles	4	4	2	4
Trolls	3	4	1	3

The second part of the Initial Data Area contains the real meat of the model, the cross rating of each alternative by each criteria. When the user has completed the entry of this data, the model can grind out a conclusion.

Decision model

"MUST" OBJECTIVES		CHOICES				
		Nort...	Easton	Southin...	Westerly	
Questing Beast		1	1	0	1	
Maiden in distress		1	1	1	1	
Holy relic		1	1	1	0	
						Check
"WANT" OBJECTIVES	Importance	Weighted scores				sums
Elves	10	20	20	30	40	110
Magic rings	10	10	40	10	40	100
Good camps	9	36	9	27	18	90
Smooth roads	7	7	21	14	28	70
Golden treasures	5	20	15	10	5	50
Dwarves	4	16	16	8	4	44
Friendly castles	2	8	8	4	8	28
Trolls	1	3	4	1	3	11
	Totals	120	133	104	146	503

First choice: Easton
Adverse effects of first choice(see also relative scores in initial data area):
—Be prepared for tough camping
—Try to stay at castles as much as possible
—Double check on Westerly's lack of a holy relic.

The model evaluates the data collected in the Initial Data Area and illustrates, in this case, which alternative should be chosen: Easton. (Two of our alternatives failed one or more of the "must" objectives.) The model includes a check-sum column to allow a cross check of the results. Beneath the arithmetic of the model is a written summary of the adverse consequences of the first choice. Note that one of the items in the list is a reminder to double check on the existence of a relic in Westerly. If Westerly could pass that "must" objective, it would be the most preferred choice.

Choice's bar graph:

Northumberland	120
Easton	133
Southington	104
Westerly	146

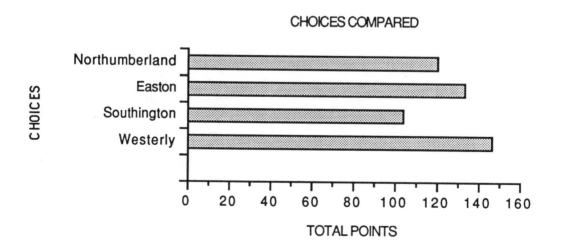

The graphing area compactly collects the data for display. The top two choices are valid, the bottom two are invalid because they failed a "must" criteria. The graph itself visually reinforces how important it is to be sure that Westerly is disqualified. It is the clear winner of the "want" criteria rating.

QUEST shows how the parts of the basic form can reinforce one another. The Introduction tells you quickly what is going on and that directions exist where you need them. The Initial Data Area supports and elaborates the Introduction with concrete data and explanatory comments. The Initial Data Area makes it easy for a new user to ask "what if" questions with this model. Finally, the directions make it possible for a new user not only to modify the present model, but to completely revise it to make a new decision. The next model, LADY, illustrates a version the Queen developed to choose a new lady in waiting.

THE MODEL "LADY"

Queen Elizabeth wanted a new lady-in-waiting with diplomatic talents. She had had some success in modifying other tools of her husband to suit her own needs, so she renamed a version of QUEST and set to work. First she set down her goal and reexamined the Introduction to alter other details as needed. Because most of the introduction was a generic description, she quickly completed this initial work.

LADY   16 November 1495   Queen Elizabeth of York

Choose a lady-in-waiting who will have diplomatic talents.

Decide which choice best satisfies several required and desired objectives.
List the choices, then list and weight the objectives to be met. Rank the choices against each other and pick the choice with the highest weighted score.

Reference: Kepner, Charles H., and Tregoe, Benjamin B., "The New Rational Manager,"
Princeton, NJ: Princeton Research Press, 1981, pp. 83-102.

Contents: (each section is a named range)
INTRO   Introduction: Title, description, contents, and directions.
INITIAL   Initial data and beginning assumptions
MODEL   Decision model
GRAPH   Choice's bar graph.

Directions:
  In the initial comments area:
    1. State the decision and the desired result.
  In the initial assumptions area:
    2. Put in choices and make comments.
    3. Enter "must" objectives—things that must be satisfied.
    4. Enter "want" objectives—things that you would like to have.
    5. Weight the importance of the "want" objectives and comment.
    6. Rate or rank the choices against each objectives.
       For example, rate the best choice (of four) as 4 and let the others have 3, 2, or 1.
       You may have ties if you wish. You may rate a choice 0 if you wish.
  In the decision model
    7. Examine the model's results and graph.
    8. Revise and reexamine the importance of objectives, the rank of choices, and other features to be sure of your choice.
    9. List the adverse consequences of the best choice to see if it will work.

Because the model was new to her, the Queen spent a good deal of time going over the fundamental rules to be sure she understood how to use it herself. She read the "must" objectives and the "want" objectives of the King, and spent a good deal of time making and revising her own list for her lady-in-waiting. She also spent considerable time deciding who the likely candidates were. When she had completed her homework, she entered her results in the first part of the Initial Data Area.

Initial data and beginning assumptions

DECISION AND RESULT:

Choose a lady-in-waiting who will have diplomatic talents.

CHOICES	COMMENTS
Jane	Beautiful, English, skilled at music, wealthy family.
Kate	English, of good family, skilled at poetry.
Anne	Stunning, skilled in languages, French, poor family.
Mary	German, wealthy family, exquisite manners.

"MUST" OBJECTIVES	COMMENTS
Noble blood	To be a lady at court, she must be from a noble family.
Speaks English	She must speak English fluently (if she is from the continent).

"WANT" OBJECTIVES		IMPORTANCE AND COMMENTS
Good looks	10	To be effective, she must be stunning.
Money	9	She should bring money when she comes to court.
Spanish	7	Able to understand important visitors.
French	7	Able to understand important visitors.
Table manners	6	Because so many gatherings are around meals.
Music	4	Able to play an instrument, sing, and dance.
Poetry	4	Accomplishment becoming a lady.
Needlework	1	A skill I must say I considered, but do not value highly.

Her four choices were two English ladies, Jane and Kate, French Anne, and German Mary. Each had her charms.

The Queen's "must" objectives had to include noble blood and fluent English. Nobility was required to gain access to the influential lords. They did not care whether a lady was of high or low nobility, but she could not, by custom, be admitted to their social affairs if not of pedigreed birth. Fluency in English was an absolute requirement for a person who would be used to influence diplomatic gatherings. The subtle shades of the language must be understood. Of course it was also desirable to be fluent in other languages for similar reasons.

Among the Queen's "want" criteria, good looks was the only traditional feminine virtue to be of much value. Money and ability with languages counted for more than the traditional accomplishments of a lady. Traditional accomplishments, however, could not be wholly ignored, and together they might outweigh some of the more sober virtues.

The next part was hard for the Queen. She rated and re-rated her four choices on her ten criteria. The "musts" were easy, but the eight "want" objectives were time-consuming. After several tries she was finally satisfied she had done as much as she could to get it right.

	Jane	Kate	Anne	Mary
Noble blood	1	1	1	1
Speaks English	1	1	1	1
		Relative scores		
Good looks	3	3	4	2
Money	3	2	1	4
Spanish	2	0	4	2
French	4	4	4	0
Table manners	1	3	4	4
Music	4	2	2	2
Poetry	1	4	3	2
Needlework	3	3	4	1

All four met the "must" criteria. Among the other criteria, Anne was the poorest, but the most beautiful, Mary, the richest, but plain, Jane and Kate were in between. French Anne, however, was a master of several languages—among the four choices she was the strongest in Spanish and French. The four's skills in traditional accomplishments were varied.

The Queen examined the results of her evaluation with great interest.

Decision model

"MUST" OBJECTIVES		CHOICES			
		Jane	Kate	Anne	Mary
Noble blood		1	1	1	1
Speaks English		1	1	1	1

"WANT" OBJECTIVES	Importance	Weighted scores				Checksums
Good looks	10	30	30	40	20	120
Money	9	27	18	9	36	90
Spanish	7	14	0	28	14	56
French	7	28	28	28	0	84
Table manners	6	6	18	24	24	72
Music	4	16	8	8	8	40
Poetry	4	4	16	12	8	40
Needlework	1	3	3	4	1	11
Totals		128	121	153	111	513

French Anne won hands down. The checksum column was clear, so no errors had crept into her reworking of her husband's model. Anne won on her looks, her language skills, and her better-than-average mastery of the traditional accomplishments of a lady. The Queen studied the results for a while to be sure she had been fair to each candidate. Then she made a list of the adverse consequences of her first choice.

Adverse effects of first choice (see also relative scores in initial data area):
—Lady Anne will not bring a strong dowry to court.
—This means that the treasury will be poorer than anticipated this year.
—Must find another means of raising some money.

The Queen knew how to deal with raising money. In order to secure the approval of her husband, she followed his example and graphed the results of LADY.

Choice's bar graph:

Jane	128
Kate	121
Anne	153
Mary	111

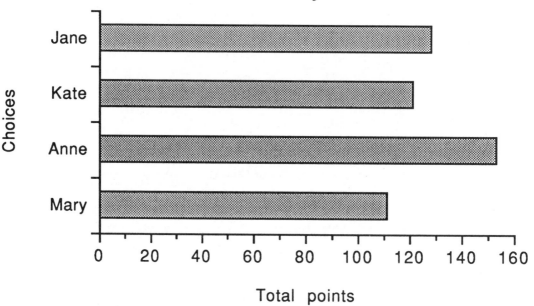

Anne is the lady of choice

The King gave his approval. As the original author, he was pleased that the Queen had used his model to such good effect. He understood her decision and could explain it to the English fathers of Jane and Kate. The Queen offered Anne the job as her new lady-in-waiting. Anne was a huge success.

THE MODEL "SEASON"

When figures vary on a regular basis over the course of a year, a common way to look for the trend in the data is to seasonally adjust the figures. When you try to look beyond the last known figure, often you fit a line through the seasonally adjusted points and figure the next month off the line. Sometimes the figure is unadjusted to find out what next month's actual result is predicted to be. The model SEASON does just that. Its result is a graph.

September sales predicted from seasonally adjusted data

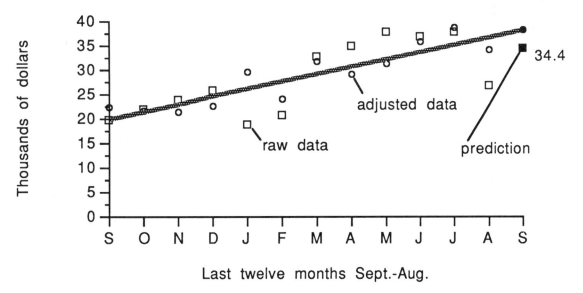

Last twelve months Sept.-Aug.

The result of SEASON contains the raw data of the last twelve months, the seasonally adjusted data, the best-fit line, and the projections for next month's figure. If you look closely at the raw data you will see that it fluctuates over the year.

This fluctuation is confirmed by the seasonal factors that are computed from the four back years of data.

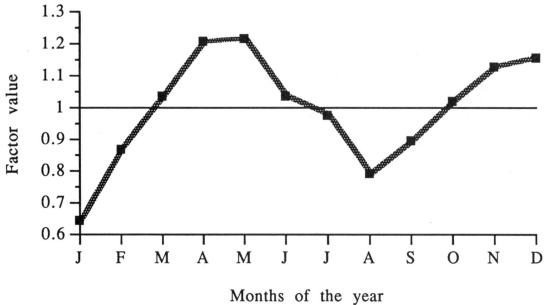

Seasonal factor for each month of the year

The year begins low and works to a high in April, declines through the summer, then rises toward a second high in December. The seasonal effect is pronounced.
   The spreadsheet SEASON starts off with no surprises.

SEASON   28 August 1640   J. Sprat

Predict next month's figure by using a best-fit line through seasonally adjusted data.

The seasonal adjustment is made using factors computed from four prior years of monthly data.

Contents: (each section is a named range)

Initial data and beginning assumptions

	1Yr	2Yr	3Yr	4Yr	This year
January	10	10	12	15	19
February	14	15	17	17	21
March	16	19	19	21	33
April	18	20	23	27	35
May	20	21	22	25	38
June	16	20	19	20	37
July	15	19	18	19	38
August	13	15	15	14	27
September	11	17	18	20	
October	13	20	20	22	
November	14	22	23	24	
December	15	21	23	26	

The Introduction and the Initial Data Area together quickly locate the reader and show him or her that the Model Area will do its work in two parts. The initial data shows four back years' data and the first part of the current year.

Model   Seasonal factors

Tricky formulas:
  Monthly factor = <raw monthly factor>/<average raw yearly factor>
  Seasonal factor = average(four monthly factors)

	RAW MONTHLY DATA				MONTHLY FACTORS				SEASONAL
	1Yr	2Yr	3Yr	4Yr	1Yr	2Yr	3Yr	4Yr	FACTORS
January	10	10	12	15	0.69	0.55	0.63	0.72	0.65
February	14	15	17	17	0.96	0.82	0.89	0.82	0.87
March	16	19	19	21	1.10	1.04	1.00	1.01	1.04
April	18	20	23	27	1.23	1.10	1.21	1.30	1.21
May	20	21	22	25	1.37	1.15	1.15	1.20	1.22
June	16	20	19	20	1.10	1.10	1.00	0.96	1.04
July	15	19	18	19	1.03	1.04	0.94	0.91	0.98
August	13	15	15	14	0.89	0.82	0.79	0.67	0.79
September	11	17	18	20	0.75	0.93	0.94	0.96	0.90
October	13	20	20	22	0.89	1.10	1.05	1.06	1.02
November	14	22	23	24	0.96	1.21	1.21	1.15	1.13
December	15	21	23	26	1.03	1.15	1.21	1.25	1.16
Average	14.6	18.2	19.1	20.8	1.00	1.00	1.00	1.00	1.00

The first part of the Model Area computes the seasonal factors. The two tricky formulas are presented first, followed by the calculations laid out from leftmost initial data to rightmost final result. The reader can methodically step across the page and follow the calculations at each step. Every factor column reiterates its formula in the bottom "Average" row where the correct answer 1.00 reassures the reader that the calculation is, in fact, correct.

After calculating the seasonal factors, the model turns its attention to projecting next month's figure.

Project next month's figure
                    The twelve months begin in September.

Fit a line to a set of points $(x(i),s(i))$, where each $s(i)$ is the seasonally adjusted version of $y(i)$. Use the line to predict the succeeding point, $s(13)$, and seasonally unadjust it to find $y(13)$.

(For details on the line-fitting calculation see the model LINEFIT in "Executive Computing: How to Get It Done with Spreadsheets and Graphs," by John M. Nevison, Atlanta, GA: AMCEE, 1986.)

Tricky formulas:
 $s(i) = y(i)/$ <seasonal factor for month>
 Each $x' = x(i) -$ average $x(i)$
 Each $s' = s(i) -$ average $s(i)$
 Slope of line, $M = $ sum$(x'*s')/$sum$(x'*x')$
 Intercept of line, $B = $ <average $s(i)$> $- M *$ <average $x(i)$>
 Best fit line $= M * x(i) + B$
 Seasonally adjusted predicted month $= M * 13 + B$
 Raw predicted month $= $ <seasonally adjusted predicted month> $*$ <seasonally factor for month>

	x(i)	y(i)	SEASONAL FACTORS	s(i)	CALCULATIONS x'	s'	x'*s'	x'*x'	BEST FIT LINE
September	1	20	0.90	22.3	−5.5	−6.2	33.91	30.25	20.1
October	2	22	1.02	21.5	−4.5	−6.9	31.26	20.25	21.6
November	3	24	1.13	21.2	−3.5	−7.2	25.30	12.25	23.1
December	4	26	1.16	22.5	−2.5	−6.0	15.01	6.25	24.6
January	5	19	0.65	29.4	−1.5	1.0	−1.46	2.25	26.2
February	6	21	0.87	24.1	−0.5	−4.4	2.19	0.25	27.7
March	7	33	1.04	31.9	0.5	3.4	1.71	0.25	29.2
April	8	35	1.21	29.0	1.5	0.5	0.78	2.25	30.7
May	9	38	1.22	31.2	2.5	2.7	6.81	6.25	32.3
June	10	37	1.04	35.7	3.5	7.2	25.27	12.25	33.8
July	11	38	0.98	38.7	4.5	10.3	46.22	20.25	35.3
August	12	27	0.79	34.1	5.5	5.6	30.80	30.25	36.8
Average	6.5			28.5	Sums	217.8	143.0		

$$1.52 = M$$
$$18.56 = B$$

Equation :   y = 1.52 * x + 18.56
Seasonally adjusted predicted month:
         x = 13   y = 38.4
Predicted month:
              34.4   0.90 Seasonal factor

This part begins with some words of introduction, followed by another set of tricky formulas. The deeper explanation of the computations is deferred to a formal reference, but the details of what the formulas are is revealed in the model. The numbers are arranged, again, in a left to right progression across the page, arriving at the coordinates of the best-fit line on the right edge.

Below the first pass of calculations, the details of the predicted month, Month 13, unfold. The predicted point on the line is 38.4, and the seasonally unadjusted figure is 34.4.

After the model has finished its computational work, it must arrange its results in a way convenient to graph.

Graphing section:
1. "Next month's sales"
2. "Seasonal factors"

	Next month's sales							Seasonal factors	
x-label	x(i)	y(i)	s(i)	Line	s(13)	y(13)	x-label		
S	1	20	22.3	20.1			J	0.65	1
O	2	22	21.5	21.6			F	0.87	1
N	3	24	21.2	23.1			M	1.04	1
D	4	26	22.5	24.6			A	1.21	1
J	5	19	29.4	26.2			M	1.22	1
F	6	21	24.1	27.7			J	1.04	1
M	7	33	31.9	29.2			J	0.98	1
A	8	35	29.0	30.7			A	0.79	1
M	9	38	31.2	32.3			S	0.90	1
J	10	37	35.7	33.8			O	1.02	1
J	11	38	38.7	35.3			N	1.13	1
A	12	27	34.1	36.8			D	1.16	1
S	13			38.4	38.4	34.4			

The Graphing Area takes advantage of its space to list the graphs by name, to set up a column of labels for the graph of the most recent twelve months, to reserve special columns for s(13) and y(13), and a column of all ones to draw a line through the center of a set of factors. Exactly how each of these columns work is unimportant. What is important is that the Graphing Area allows the author enough room to create exactly the right graph. The graph remains the most important element of this spreadsheet.

THE MODEL "TIMELY"

When a planner with several chores looks at the uncertainty associated with any one of them, it may seem as if the whole project is in real danger of never getting done. Actually, just the opposite is true: if you can estimate the parts of a job well, the whole job is easier to estimate. In the spreadsheet TIMELY, King Henry puts together a model to help him estimate the length of time it might take to gain control of a neighboring kingdom.

The beginning of the spreadsheet introduces the reader to the method employed.

TIMELY   ACTIVITIES   14 Sept 1521   King Henry
(C) Copyright 1986 by John M. Nevison

Estimate the project completion time from the estimates of the component activities.

The component activities are serial—one must be completed before the next is begun. In a large project these activities all lie on the critical path.

To use:
1. Count your tasks—each should depend on the one before.
2. If you need more tasks, insert copies of an old task row in the middle of the list;
   if fewer, delete a few rows from the middle of the list.
3. Enter the name, low, likely, and high estimates for your tasks.
4. Adjust the model to the size of your initial data.

Contents: (each section is a named range)
 INTRO   Introduction:Title, description, contents.
 INITIAL Initial data and beginning assumptions
 MODEL   Model
 REPORT   Report area
 GRAPH   Graph area

The instructions emphasize the requirement that the tasks follow one another and that each depend on the one before. Two sets of tasks that have these properties are the tasks on a critical path of a large project and the tasks you, as an individual, set out to do on any given day. (Many times some of the personal tasks may be independent, but if they all must be finished by one person, the set's time requirements behave as if the individual tasks were serially dependent.)

Initial data and beginning assumptions
  -Low has a 1/1000 chance of happening—very optimistic estimate, everything goes right.
  -High has a 1/1000 chance of happening—extremely pessimistic estimate, everything goes completely wrong.
  -Likely is the most likely single estimate (the mode), everything is completely normal.

Task name	Low	Likely	High
Make nails	8	10	20
Make shoes	5	15	30
Shoe horses	4	8	15
Train riders	5	10	25
Win battles	21	35	180
Gain kingdom	20	30	60

The Initial Data Area has some reminders that help the user enter the right kind of estimates for each task. King Henry estimated his tasks. The first two make use of his blacksmith shop. He must make nails before he can make shoes. After the manufacturing is complete the same smith must shoe all the horses. If his cousin can learn the job and work a second shift each day, and if his cousin is good, the job will proceed quickly; if either smith gets sick, the job will be slowed. Because of the new shoes, the riders must train themselves and their mounts for battle. Winning a battle involves finding the foe and engaging him (victory is assumed). Whether the foe stands and fights or runs and must be cornered leads to great uncertainty in the time it will take to conclude a major victory in battle. The formalities of assuming the crown could be accomplished in three weeks, but if the ceremonies must wait on the attendance of certain visiting royalty, they might be delayed several weeks.

When he had finished entering the initial data, the King turned his attention to the model itself.

Model
Tricky formulas:
  Expected = (low + 4*likely + high)/6
  Standard deviation = (high − low)/6
  Variance = (standard deviation)^2
  Project standard deviation = square root(project variance)

Task name	Low	Likely	High	Expected	Variance	
Make nails	8	10	20	11.3	4.0	
Make shoes	5	15	30	15.8	17.4	
Shoe horses	4	8	15	8.5	3.4	
Train riders	5	10	25	11.7	11.1	
Win battles	21	35	180	56.8	702.2	
Gain kingdom	20	30	60	33.3	44.4	
						Standard deviation
Project totals				137.5	782.5	28.0
Check sums	63	108	330	137.5		

The model itself begins with a list of the tricky formulas employed in the calculations. With their help the King can see how his individual task estimates were combined into an estimate for the whole project. He examines the results closely because he doesn't believe it should take so long. After reviewing the individual tasks, confirming to himself that the individual tasks could not be doubled up, and reviewing how this project compared to the last one like it, he decides the estimate is accurate.

He checks his old Report Area and Graphing Area to see if they still work.

Report area
    26-Nov-21   ESTIMATED PROJECT COMPLETION TIME
           6   Number of activities on the project critical path
       137.5   Project mean completion time (50-50 chance)
        28.0   Project completion time standard deviation

		PROJECT COMPLETION TIME TABLE				
	Time:	82	118	138	157	193
Probability:		2%	24%	50%	76%	98%

Graph area
"Timely's completion time": the project probable completion time

Std. devs	Curve	Prob.	Times
−3.00	0.02	0.1%	54
−2.50	0.07	0.6%	
−2.00	0.21	2.3%	
−1.50	0.51	6.7%	96
−1.00	0.95	15.9%	
−0.50	1.39	30.9%	
0.00	1.57	50.0%	138
0.50	1.39	69.1%	
1.00	0.95	84.1%	
1.50	0.51	93.3%	179
2.00	0.21	97.7%	
2.50	0.07	99.4%	
3.00	0.02	99.9%	221

After he looks at them for a few minutes he remembers that they both depend on only three numbers from the Model Area: the number of tasks, the project mean, and project standard deviation. The answers appear correct.

Finally he calls up the graph called "Timely's completion time."

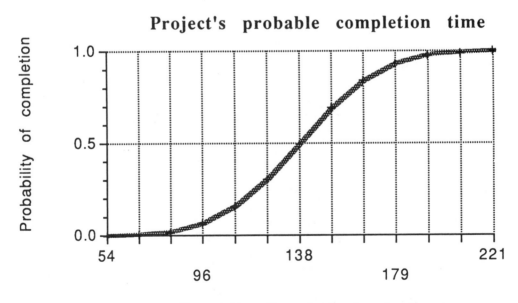

Project's probable completion time

Probability of completion

Completion time (calendar days)

The curve tells him the campaign will be over in four to six months. The model tells him the campaign's completion depends heavily on how fast he can engage the enemy. After he prints out copies for his files, he saves a copy of the model for later adjustment as the project unfolds.

To save a general tool that he can use later on another project, the King enters an appropriate set of initial test data and checks the model to be sure it correctly manipulates those data.

Task name	Low	Likely	High	Expected	Variance	
Activity 1	2	5	14	6.0	4.0	
Activity 2	2	5	14	6.0	4.0	
Activity 3	2	5	14	6.0	4.0	
Activity 4	2	5	14	6.0	4.0	
Activity 5	2	5	14	6.0	4.0	
Activity 6	2	5	14	6.0	4.0	
Activity 7	2	5	14	6.0	4.0	
Activity 8	2	5	14	6.0	4.0	
Activity 9	2	5	14	6.0	4.0	
						Standard deviation
Project totals				54.0	36.0	6.0

The answers are correct. He saves this version of the model for his next project and goes to bed.

6

THE WIDER WORLD

GOING TO ST. IVES

As I was going to St. Ives
I met a man with seven wives.
Every wife had seven sacks,
Every sack had seven cats,
Every cat had seven kits.
Kits, cats, sacks, and wives,
How many were going to St. Ives?

Sometimes even while you are building a spreadsheet, you know it is destined for others to use. You know that when your work goes public, it will suffer the trials and tribulations of the wider world.

The wider world asks you to extend your concern for the reader and user of your work. The wider world is, unfortunately, a more uncertain world. It is uncertain about who will use your work, about how he or she will use it, and about who may eventually change it. This uncertainty grows worse as the future's horizon recedes. As the author of the spreadsheet, you must acknowledge this uncertainty, but you need not entirely surrender to it. What you owe to the future's wider world is your best guess of likely alternatives and your prudent attention to those present details that may have future consequences.

The goal of all spreadsheet activity is better decisions. The decision maker who will be using your spreadsheet needs a spreadsheet that works *correctly*. One of the ways your behavior will change as you prepare for the wider world is that you will do more to convince the eventual user that your spreadsheet is, and will remain, correct.

THE WORK GROUP AND ITS CONCERNS

A good framework for thinking about the concerns of the wider world is to imagine a work group of four to seven people who will use your spreadsheet, and to imagine the environment they will be working in. Anticipate and forestall as many of their problems as possible. You should revisit each of the areas of your spreadsheet and test it against the work group's needs.

The results of your revisit may mean further work on your spreadsheet. Past experience indicates getting a spreadsheet ready to go public is hard work. *Be prepared to spend as much time revising to go public as you spent writing.*

Because correctness is the major concern, a Verify Area becomes a must for all but the most simple spreadsheets. Even in a simple spreadsheet, defensive formulas that set off "error" warnings should be employed wherever possible. The future user who sees a spreadsheet with a Verify Area and columns labeled "check sums" has visible evidence of the original author's commitment to a correct spreadsheet.

The work group's needs require that the Model Area meet the highest standards of clarity. If the user cannot understand what the model does, he or she will be reluctant to use it. Someone once said, "A person would rather live with a problem he cannot solve than adopt a solution he does not understand." Be sure that your model's equations will be clear to the average reader in the work group, not just the brightest reader.

The reports and graphs were originally designed for a specific audience and will probably need no revision. Remember, however, that someone in the work group will be maintaining these areas, and review your instructions to be sure they are clear and complete.

The Active Area and the Macro Area may get completely reworked after you seriously consider the work group's use of your model. When you carefully review which parts of the model will be used frequently and which will not be used much at all, you may wish to smooth the user's path with an Active Area or an appropriate macro. When you add these features, you must also go the second mile and provide sufficient explanations and instructions so that an average user will not only be convinced of the activity's correctness, but will feel confident that he or she can modify the model appropriately and maintain its correctness.

A potent weapon in your arsenal is the submodel. When you can match a submodel to a work group activity that you anticipate may change over time, you will ensure that the changes to the model can be carried out in a contained area. By isolating the area likely to change, you protect the rest of the spreadsheet from unnecessary disturbances. The portion that is not disturbed will not have errors introduced into it.

After you have reworked the body of the spreadsheet to meet the work group's needs, you will return to the Initial Data Area and the Introduction. Here you will need the help of the real, or imaginary, spreadsheet library and its librarian.

THE LIBRARIAN'S REQUIREMENTS

The spreadsheet librarian is the individual responsible for enforcing the work group's standards on the spreadsheet. Even if you have neither work group standards nor a librarian, pretend for the moment that both exist and review your program from that point of view.

Ask yourself what the standards of a librarian might be. Here is a possible checklist:

- Everything in the basic spreadsheet introduction
   - Title, date, name of author
   - Alterations, date, name of reviser
   - Purpose
   - Directions
   - References
   - Contents and map
- Special details on how this fits with work group practices and procedures:
   - Telephone numbers of people who will answer questions about this spreadsheet
   - Supporting documents, files, procedures, or people
- External documentation (if the spreadsheet is one of a system of spreadsheets)
- Details of the supporting technical environment, including:
   - The computer the spreadsheet will run on
   - The operating system the spreadsheet will run on
   - The software the spreadsheet will run on

> The disk (physical location and name) that contains the spreadsheet
> The file folder (physical location and name) with the paper copies of the spreadsheet
> • Operating limitations
>   Who the assumed user is
>   What the assumed user knows
>   When and how the spreadsheet should be used
>   When the spreadsheet should *not* be used
>   Warnings and cautionary notes

Working through this checklist and being sure that your completed Introduction addresses it will enhance your spreadsheet's contribution to your work group's real productivity. Remember that what you write once will be read by many readers: common courtesy requires that you anticipate your readers' likely questions and answer them before they ask.

The above list can affect the way you arrange and describe your Initial Data and whether or not you wish to include an Input Area in your spreadsheet. Make sure your Initial Data gives the user a strong foundation of confidence in the whole spreadsheet.

If your work group has not set up standards and practices for spreadsheets yet is using them quite heavily, you may want to initiate the discussion about what standards might make sense. Retain your sense of humour and proportion when you set up these standards, and be prepared to revise them in the light of your collective experience.

If your work group has a set of standards for spreadsheets, it probably already has an informal library of spreadsheets in a central location. That library should require at least three things of any spreadsheet that wishes to be considered for inclusion:

• A disk with the spreadsheet (or system of spreadsheets) on it—and a second, backup disk.
• A full printed copy of each spreadsheet with a set of data that helps explain how the spreadsheet works.
• A second, complete, printed copy of each spreadsheet that shows all formulas in full as they are arranged on the spreadsheet.

FINAL MOVES

After you have completed revising your spreadsheet for the wider world, give it a few final reality checks. Because the spreadsheet faces the challenge of explaining itself to an uninformed user, it must be reviewed by someone other than the original author before it is approved for use. To get the most out of this review, give the model to at least two readers and, if possible, include the intended user as one of these readers. If the spreadsheet will be used by several people, include as many of them as possible as reviewers.

Listen to your proofreaders' comments. Incorporate improvements that you think will answer their criticisms and return the spreadsheet to them for review. After your readers think they understand the printed spreadsheet, ask one of them to make mock use of it—to take it out for a test drive. The user may vary an assumption and play "what if?" with the model. The user may add another month's data to the Initial Data. The user may simulate the end-of-the-year activity when the model's data must be stored and the model revised for a whole new year. The user can try an independent set of Initial Data to see if the spreadsheet really works. The more test use the model gets, the better your final spreadsheet will be.

After you believe you have done everything that can be done to prepare your spreadsheet for the wider world, you must temporarily assume the role of spreadsheet librarian. Take your spreadsheet as an author and set it down on the desk. Walk around the desk. Pick the spreadsheet up as the librarian. Perform the librarian's review of the spreadsheet vigorously, even though the author in you may not like what it hears. After you have completed the librarian's review, set the results back down on the desk. Walk around the desk the other way, and see how you did as an author. Repeat this exercise until both of you are satisfied with the results.

You will be finished when you can look at your work and say to yourself, "I would be happy to use this spreadsheet." Remember Solomon's remark that "time and chance happeneth to them all": someday you may find yourself the surprised user of your own work. Make the user in you grateful to the author in you.

R E F E R E N C E S

Nevison, John M. *The Little Book of BASIC Style: How to Write a Program You Can Read*. Reading, MA: Addison-Wesley, 1978.

This work contains details on problem solving and a clear introduction to computer programming. The references at the back of the book point the reader to an excellent collection of books and articles about computer programming.

Nevison, John M. *Executive Computing: How to Get It Done on Your Own*. Reading, MA: Addison-Wesley, 1981.

This work presents case studies about a variety of business ideas. The studies all use computer programs written in BASIC. References at the end of each chapter point the reader to a wide array of business applications. Appendix A gives a brief explanation of structured programming.

Nevison, John M. *Executive Computing: How to Get It Done with Spreadsheets and Graphs*. Atlanta, GA: Association for Media-Based Continuing Education for Engineers, 1986.

The revised version of the previous work contains spreadsheets and graphs instead of computer programs. The case studies explain the business ideas. References at the end of each chapter point the reader to a wide array of business applications.

Simon, Herbert. *The Sciences of the Artificial*. Cambridge, MA: MIT Press, 1969.

This is a collection of lectures by a man who is a distinguished management scientist (Nobel Prize in Economics) and an outstanding computer scientist (Turning Award). The talks are a thought-provoking and informative introduction to the problems of design.

Strunk, William, Jr., and White, E.B. *The Elements of Style*. 3rd ed. New York: Macmillan, 1979.

  The second book to read when you want to write good spreadsheets. The first book to read when you want to write.

Tufte, Edward R. *The Visual Display of Quantitative Information*. Cheshire, CT: Graphics Press, 1983.

  The third book to read when you want to write good spreadsheets. The first book to read when you want to display quantitative information.

Zeisel, Hans. *Say It with Figures*. 5th ed. rev., New York: Harper & Row, 1968.

  This work is a classic in the field of social science analysis. Read it when you want to know how to get to the root causes of business activity—how to ask the questions and how to look at the answers.

APPENDIX: CHECKLISTS FOR ACTION

This appendix is intended to give you step-by-step, generic instructions on several small but important techniques you may employ in your spreadsheet work. The phrasing is heavily influenced by the commands of Lotus 1-2-3™, Version 1A. Before following any of these lists, check the manual of your spreadsheet to be sure of the syntax for the appropriate commands.

HOW TO LINK CELLS

Suppose that the value 10% is in the cell A1 on a spreadsheet. Ten percent represents the percentage interest that your firm is using in its financial models. You wish to use this figure at several other locations on your spreadsheet, in particular in cell B20.
   To link cell B20 to A1:

1. Go to cell B20.
2. Enter the formula +A1.
3. Check your work by varying the value in A1 and be sure the value in B20 varies accordingly.

To link a block of cells, for example the six-cell block A1..B3, to another block of cells:

1. Go to the upper left corner of the new area (for example, B51).
2. Link upper left corners (B51 and A1).
3. Copy the new formula in the upper left corner, B51, into the block B51..D53 .
4. Check the results to be sure the formulas in the new block are correct. When you are done

A1..B3 might contain: and look like:

.10	.12	.15		10%	12%	15%
8	5	10		8.0	5.0	10.0

and B51..D53 would contain: and look like:

+A1	+A2	+A3		10%	12%	15%
+B1	+B2	+B3		8.0	5.0	10.0

By linking single cells or whole blocks of cells, you can link parts of a Model Area to the values in the Initial Data Area. When you link to a single value, you will probably want it to be an absolute reference. When you link to the upper left corner of a block, column, or row of cells, you will probably want the reference to be relative so you can copy the formula from the new left corner into the whole new block.

HOW TO FIX AN OLD SPREADSHEET

When you are confronted by an old spreadsheet that you want to fix:

1. Study it and decide what single area it most resembles. If it is primarily raw data with almost no formulas, it resembles an Initial Data Area. If it is a thicket of formulas, it resembles a Model Area.
2. Import your whole old spreadsheet into the appropriate area of a fresh template like FULL RULE.
3. Rename it and save it under its new name.
4. Systematically work through the old spreadsheet and move items to the appropriate areas. Raw data goes in the Initial Data Area, formal introductions go in the Introduction, title line goes at the top of the Introduction, and so on.
5. Using the template as a guide, add new introductory features that your old spreadsheet lacked. You may begin with the title line, you probably will need a table of contents, and you may wish to improve your references and your directions.

6. Continuing to use the template as your guide, build areas that need to be added. A Verify Area can be a big help. You may need a Report Area or a Graphing Area.
7. Erase extraneous template material from your results.
8. Unprotect appropriate areas and protect everything else.
9. Test your results to be sure they are correct.
10. Save the result and consider it a possible template for some of your future work.

HOW TO PROTECT YOUR SPREADSHEET

Spreadsheet commands provide a variety of ways to "protect" a cell. The general effect of this protection is that the user is prevented from inadvertently altering the contents. Some spreadsheets actually provide protection schemes that allow the author to use a password to lock up a cell.

These protection schemes are good first lines of defense. They should not, however, be mistaken for more than they are. They are not insurance that no one will change your spreadsheet. They are not a guarantee that no one will accidentally alter your sheet. (The first user can turn the protection off and forget to turn it back on; the second user can make a mistake moving data around.) They are not an excuse to fail to document the whole spreadsheet. ("Because this is protected the user doesn't have to understand it" is a bad excuse.)

In fact, protection schemes offer so little protection you should treat your spreadsheets as if they were going to be handled in an unprotected fashion. Do protect them wherever possible; just don't kid yourself about how much protection you have purchased.

When you protect:

1. Begin by unprotecting those areas you wish to allow the user to change. By unprotecting you force yourself to think about each area you wish to open, and you err on the side of overprotecting the spreadsheet when you forget something.
2. Turn on protection for the whole spreadsheet. (Read your manual to learn the details of how to do this.)

3. If your spreadsheet has a password feature, use it.
4. Test the spreadsheet to be sure you have correctly protected it.

HOW TO PRINT A SPREADSHEET AS FORMULAS

If you are preparing a paper copy of your work for your files, you will want to have a copy of your spreadsheet with the formulas in their proper location in the spreadsheet. Because some of your formulas may be long, the columns they appear in will necessarily be wide. In fact, be prepared for the formula version of your spreadsheet to be quite large.

You may purchase various programs to print the formulas in your spreadsheet. If you choose to purchase one, try it out at the store (or try a friend's copy) to be sure it works to your satisfaction.

If you are working with Lotus 1-2-3™, Version 1A, the Range Format Text command will accomplish what you want to do. Other spreadsheet programs that have appeared since 1983 accomplish this printing in various ways. Consult your manual to find out how your own spreadsheet works.

When you are ready to print your spreadsheet as formulas:

1. Call up a copy of your spreadsheet that you will either throw away or save under a separate name.
2. Use your spreadsheet commands to convert the display to all formulas. (This may involve repeated use of Range Format Text command in 1-2-3.)
3. Widen each column until all formulas in it are completely visible.
4. Print a paper copy.
5. Assemble the paper copy into one large copy and review it carefully to be sure all formulas are visible.
6. Store it with the regular printed copy of your spreadsheet.

NOTE-IT PROGRAMS

Programs that allow you to document a cell in a spreadsheet with a pop-up window can be a welcome addition to your work. They allow the author to provide the user, but not necessarily the reader, with an extra explanation of what's going on. Be sure not to let note-it programs substitute for good spreadsheet design. A good spreadsheet makes all its ideas available *to the reader* of the printed copy. As long as you continue to meet this test, you may employ note-it programs with profit.

When you use a note-it program:

1. Watch your notes as you write them.
2. When you spot one that is not just handy, but crucial, surface it in a written comment in the spreadsheet.

FUTURE PRODUCTS FOR SPREADSHEETS

Lotus Development Corporation has just announced a companion product to 1-2-3 called HAL™. The early reports (January 1987) are that this tool can substantially aid the user as he or she works with a spreadsheet.

If you make spreadsheets for others to use, you should:

1. Acquaint yourself with this enhancement (and others as they are announced).
2. Decide if, how, and where you will use its features in your work.
3. Decide how to inform the reader of a printed copy of the spreadsheet about the features you use. (Perhaps you create small remarks in various areas of the spreadsheet, perhaps you create a new area, perhaps you do both.)

I N D E X

About the Author

John M. Nevison is President of Goodmeasure Software Corporation, a firm that improves management performance through effective computer technology. The author of four related computing books, he is a past chairman of the Greater Boston Chapter of the Association for Computing Machinery. He holds a mathematics degree from Dartmouth College, and lives in Concord, MA with his wife and two daughters.